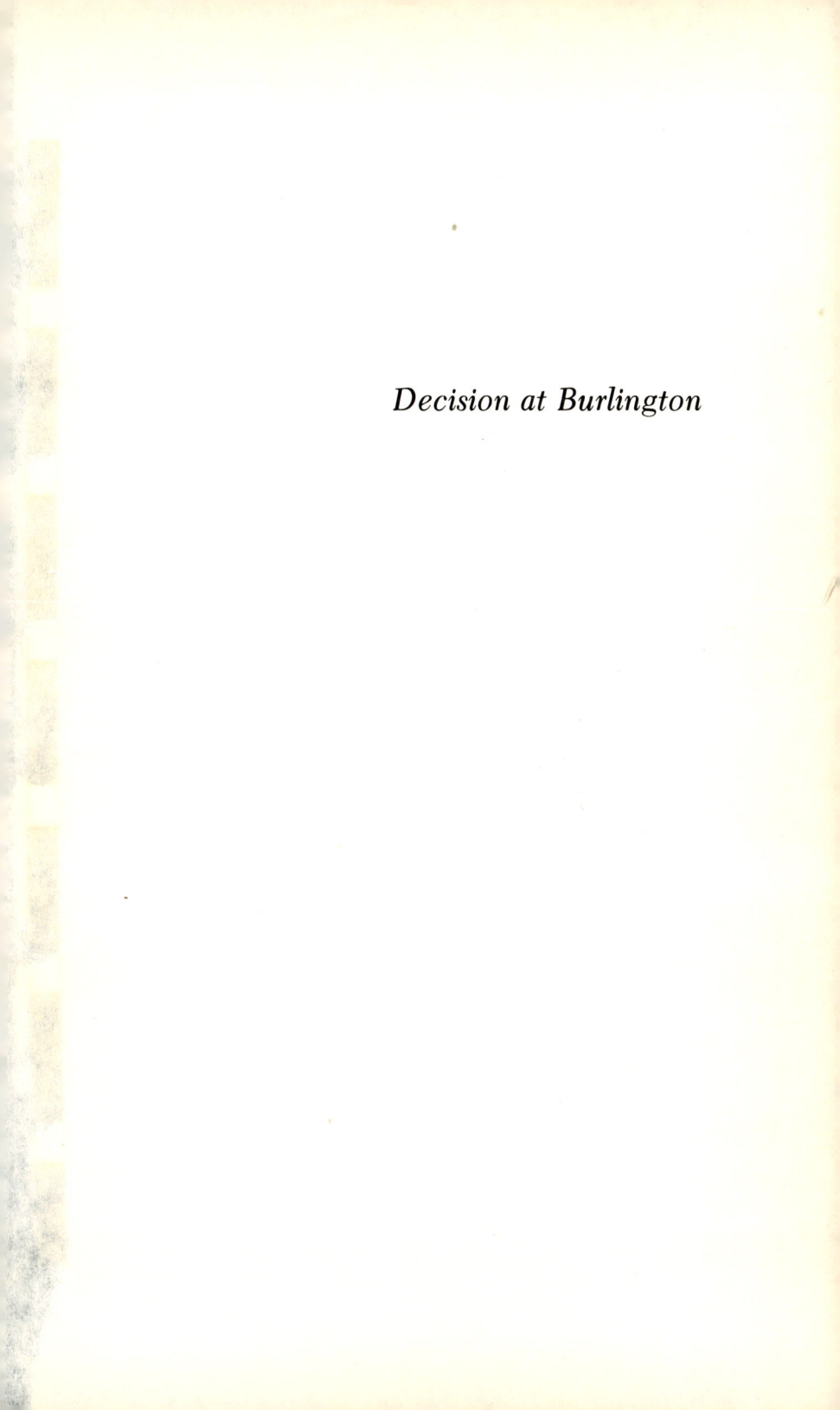

Decision at Burlington

DECISION

AT

BURLINGTON

Steve **Dolan**

North Star Press

Saint Cloud   Minnesota

Published by North Star Press, P.O. Box 451, St. Cloud, Minnesota, 56301

Copyright © F. J. Steve Dolan 1978

International Standard Book Numbers:
                        0-87839-033-2   paperback
                        0-87839-034-0   cloth binding

All rights reserved. Printed in the United States of America by Sentinel Printing Company, St. Cloud, Minnesota. Typography by Media + Materials, Inc., St. Cloud, Minnesota. Binding by Midwest Editions Inc., Minneapolis, Minnesota.

DEDICATION

to

The girls and women who take unwanted pregnancies to term, thereby providing their babies with the eventual opportunity to love God and neighbor and thus fulfill the new commandment that Jesus brought to this earth.

CONTENTS

I Chapter	1
II Chapter	9
III Chapter	22
IV Chapter	29
V Chapter	35
VI Chapter	42
VII Chapter	63
VIII Chapter	73
IX Chapter	84
X Chapter	104
XI Chapter	117
XII Chapter	140
XIII Chapter	158
XIV Chapter	168
XV Chapter	178
XVI Chapter	191
XVII Chapter	206

Decision at Burlington

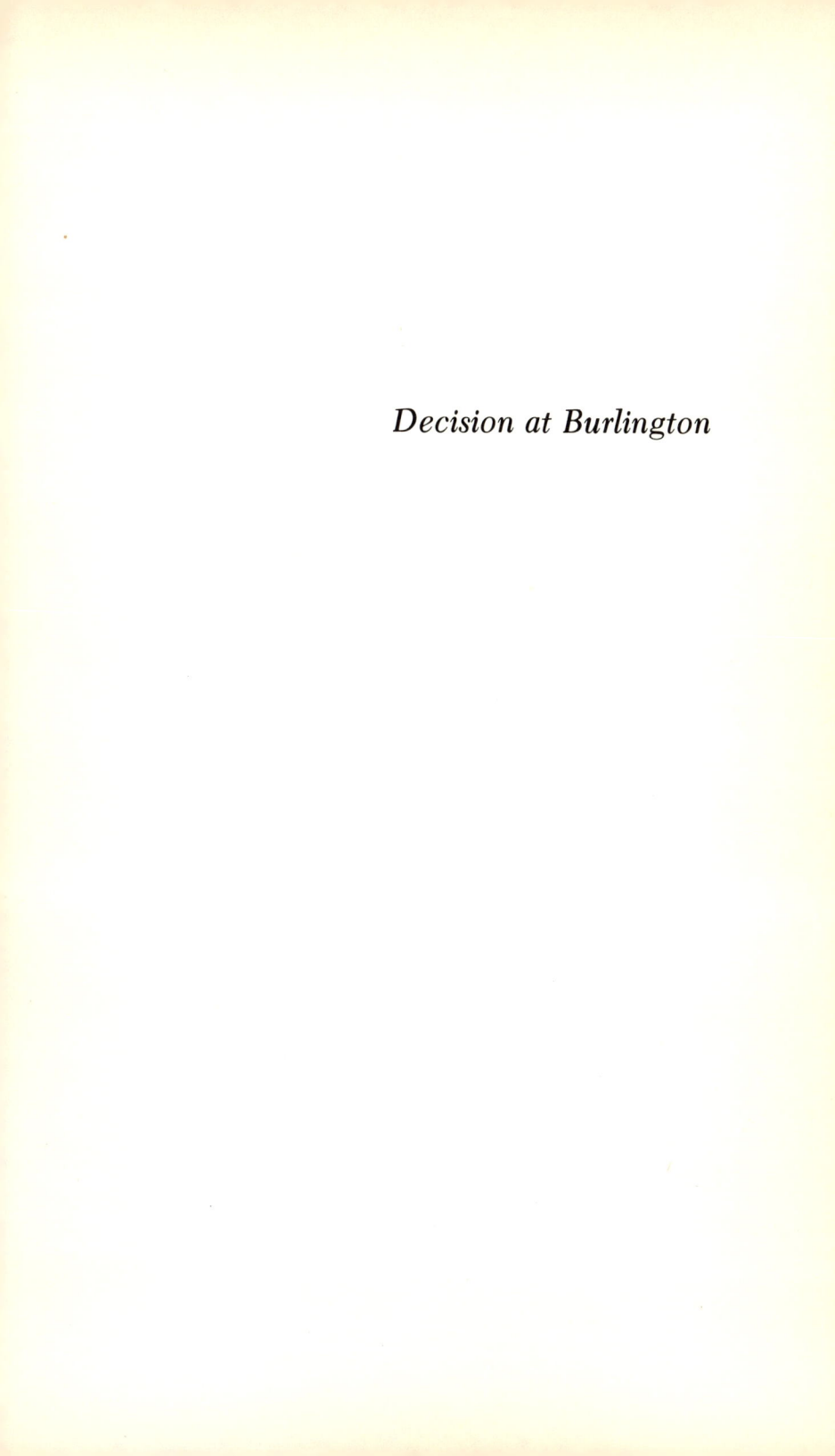

I

The desire to be mayor of Burlington was cached in my daydreams until incumbent Marcella Baker informed me of her intention to resign the office.

The first woman chief executive in the city's history was quitting in her third term because her husband's progressive alcoholism was threatening the stability of their family's enterprises.

Though she only guessed at my interest in succeeding her, Mayor Baker graciously imparted the information to me before it was made public.

An unusual contest would be held in Burlington. The city charter called for an intramural selection process by the city council for midterm vacancies in both the mayor's office and the council itself. City council members would be prohibited from choosing a peer as the new mayor. Any other registered voter or resident of the city for six months would be eligible to run.

The most senior council member would be called upon to assume the city council's presidency and conduct the election.

After heading Mrs. Baker's volunteer campaign organization before her first term, the fifty-five year old mother of four sons turned often to me in the ensuing years with questions of strategy. I enjoyed my advisory role in her administration, in part because it provided a laboratory for bills I contemplated sponsoring at the state legislature, where I was serving as a member of the House of Representatives.

Mayor Baker's accessibility, sound budgets and calm leadership impressed the electorate in this city of one and one-half million people. Nevertheless, she wasn't excited about the city of Burlington being swallowed into Jackson County, a change that voters in both entities had approved overwhelmingly at the last general election. Marcella knew the environs were populated with a different class of voters. And with her husband Harold's alcohol problem, her political zeal was gone.

The mayor left it to me to decide how many or how few persons to tell of her decision. It probably would leak out soon, she had said, and when confronted by the media, she would say merely that a statement would be issued one week hence.

My heart beat fast as I carried our secret onto the expansive, snow-covered boulevard separating City Hall from the Chaix-Gordon Hotel.

I walked slowly toward the fifty story Merchandise Mart where offices for lawyers, realtors, insurance brokers and other self-employed business persons were located in the top half of the building.

The glass-sheathed Mart loomed larger than it had in the past. I took an express elevator to the fortieth floor office of Bart Countryman, a political wizard in the county Democratic party. In the past ten years, the attorney headed several compaigns from the start and resurrected others after lackluster primary election performances. His success ratio in city and county battles was nearly perfect.

After experiencing momentary apprehension, I stepped into Countryman's paneled office and told him of my goal. I, Connor Mullaney, wanted to be mayor of Burlington and I asked Bart to appraise my chance of success.

Most urban Democrats became card-carriers because of factional concerns, such as the need for collective bargaining, or the wish to preserve the strength of the first amendment to the constitution relating to freedom of speech. The young man facing me, though, was one of those rare members of either major political party whose avocational involvement emanated from an intention simply to assist his party on a broad front.

The confession of my aspiration caused Countryman to lean far back in the leather swivel chair his ample frame filled. He showed a second sign of shock and turned to gaze out the huge window that dominated one side of his office.

Though noncommittal, he was encouraging. "I'm pleased that you're thinking of running," he said. "You are respected as a state representative. I know you ran quite well for the House, especially considering that very little money was spent on yard signs or newspaper advertising."

His manner became more demonstrative. "Your name has been mentioned occasionally as a future mayoral candidate, so I am happy you have decided to run. I might add that you're wise to start early. By the way, we're both assuming our incumbent will choose not to seek a fourth term, aren't we, Connor?"

Before I could answer, Countryman asked, "You wouldn't oppose Marcella Baker, would you?"

I decided at this juncture to inform him of Mayor Baker's confidential disclosure to me and I asked that it remain a secret. He did not appear surprised when I informed him.

As we talked, I perceived one of the reasons for which I sought out Countryman. He had a reputation for telling candidates straightforwardly whether he thought they were attractive or bland, incompetent bunglers or people with talent who could be of service to a constituency. That was why I felt comfortable with him.

Antithetically, covert character attacks expended much of the members' energy in Burlington Democratic and Republican circles. When an onslaught came from the opposition, a candidate could expect defense from all sides of his party. But when an intraparty assassin struck, the victim seldom was defended.

I couldn't accept that as a political truism until I became aware that nearly every party member had an ulterior motivation. Obstructing an internal backstabber would mean gaining at least one enemy, and when one's objective was to secure an endorsement, a committee appointment, a government job or a pork-barrel contract, one could ill-afford to offend a fellow party member.

In a lengthy meeting, Countryman and I examined the merits and shortcomings of my candidacy. He said that in the many campaigns he headed, candidates didn't have to worry about shortcomings if they were able to convince their respective electorates they were knowledgeable and honest.

Bart Countryman promised me his help in winning the intramural election. As I left his office, I agreed to an issues' discussion the next day.

— ★ ★ ★ —

The phone was ringing as I opened my apartment door. For an unexplainable reason, I knew it would be Jack Clay, my architect friend who found relief from his exacting vocation in the inexact world of politics. Fresh from helping Allard Jacobs win the governorship, Clay was enthused. "Have you heard the news?" he asked. "Marcella Baker may quit next month."

He had found out the rumor quite soon. His source could only have been one of the mayor's relatives. The Bakers and Clays were longtime members of Burlington society. Many in the two clans took seriously the obligation of the highborn to government service.

"This should be kept quiet," Clay warned. "I know the benefit of getting in ahead of the mob. We can be sure a lot of people will be after the vacancy. Some of them will even be qualified. Ah, you will think of running, won't you?"

"Yes, Jack, I've already been given a pledge of help by Bart Countryman."

"Good. I have a call in to the governor," Clay said. "I let his secretary know of Marcella's plans and said that I wanted you to meet with Allard."

There went the last shred of confidentiality. I really didn't think the secret would endure for more than a couple of days, anyway.

I had met Govenor Jacobs only once. He had returned from congress to the governorship just three months ago.

"I know Allard enjoys sticking his nose into local politics," Clay said, "so he's a natural to help; at least if I ask him."

Of course, I was pleased Jack Clay would do that for me, and I told him. But I was concerned about the strategy of seeing the governor prior to meeting with the more minor party functionaries in Burlington. Not wanting to smother his enthusiasm, however, I did not mention the dubitable value of starting at the top and working downward. It would not have made any difference, as my concern would have been lost in Jack's ebullience.

As I drove to Clay's office to await the governor's call, I remembered another reason to question the wisdom of the proposed appointment. Governor Jacobs reportedly was a faddist, and that could portend his position on abortion.

The heavy volume of traffic slowed my journey, giving me an opportunity to ponder the course I should take with Jacobs.

With the selection of Mrs. Baker's successor to take place in the council, the election could consume two days or three months. Therefore, I was unable to plan a normal campaign by laying out a chronological schedule of contacts with the city and county kingmakers. For all I knew, one visit with the governor might trigger the local union leaders to back my candidacy. And, of course, my campaign could be sabotaged with a single phone call.

As I alighted from my Chevy hardtop, Jack was waiting at the curb in front of his office building. His mood was still high. "I just spoke with Allard," he said, "and I lined up a meeting. He likes your record as a state representative and he wants to talk."

He gave me the time of the appointment and then searched my face for approbation.

"I'm appreciative of what you've done," I said, "but I want you to know that I will not change any of my stands in order to win the approval of the governor. He's so new in his first term, I don't know how he looks at several issues, some of them crucial issues, such as the right to life in the womb."

"I knew him when I was younger," Clay told me, "and then more recently, I became involved in the tail end of his gubernatorial effort. But I must say, I don't know how he *really* stands on abortion."

Jack was getting around to answering me. "Don't worry about saying anything that would damage my relationship with the governor. I'm not out for any favors from him or any other office holders."

Feeling better, I drove to another downtown office building to quiz an old classmate of Allard Jacobs.

Bernie Miller was a hard-driving realtor specializing in commercial properties. He retained a friendship with the governor, his boyhood pal, but avoided participating in his various campaigns. "Too many committees," he once told me.

Though ours was only a casual acquaintanceship, we were at ease with each other.

When Miller heard the recitation of my name to his secretary, he emerged from his office and beckoned me inward.

We discussed Mayor Baker's bombshell before I asked his opinion of the governor's true feelings on abortion.

"I believe he would take a visceral rather than intellectual approach to the subject," Miller said. "That's because of his dislike for researching a topic, but also because a girl he admired in high school died after a backstreet abortion."

In a disjointed afterthought, the realtor said, "Jacobs was only an average student when I was in school with him."

The first part of his message wasn't what I wanted to hear, but the last seemed to tell me I should stand up to the governor and not beg.

II

I AWOKE BEFORE the alarm sounded. It was good that Jack Clay had made a nine a.m. appointment, as I had less time in the day to worry.

I considered the early victories of the man I was about to see. A congressman for twelve years and governor for three months, he still was only thirty-nine years old. His record was not dazzling, though. In all of his years in congress, Allard Jacobs never chaired a committee, was always out of town during abortion votes, never authored any major legislation and seldom made any enemies, except when he flailed away at the fat cats who avoided paying income taxes. That dragon-slaying ploy was his only show of social outrage. It was loved on every rung of the endorsing caste within the state Democratic party machinery, the attritive group which gave the governor a first ballot endorsement at last summer's convention.

I drove to the eastern edge of Burlington and parked within a cluster of government buildings. From two blocks away, I could see an obelisk pointing skyward near the western apse of the state capitol. The three story marble edifice had been constructed in the late nineteenth century during the neo-baroque period, with its ostentatious sculpturing and excessive interior coloring.

The central dome rose two hundrd twenty feet, with subsidiary domes covering the House and Senate chambers. Extending unsymmetrically from the rear of the capitol, the Supreme Court wing adhered to the original, seventeenth century definition of the word "baroque," meaning a pearl that was not perfectly round.

As I mounted the worn concrete steps, I recited a prayer of St. Augustine:

> Leave the past to the mercy of God,
> The present to his love
> And the future to his providence.

The huge oaken door swung wide with little effort. I expected to see several levels of aides before encountering the governor. That's the way it had been with his predecessor.

I stopped when I arrived at the entrance to the governor's opulently furnished reception room. Solid beige drapes hung thirty feet from ceiling to baseboard. A mural of farmers shocking bundles of wheat covered an entire wall. An equally obsolescent scene of a rural cook shanty had my attention when a soft voice said, "You must be Representative Mullaney. I'm Sally Carruthers."

"How do you do."

"I just heard from the governor. He's on his way and asks your indulgence. He called from his limousine, so he shouldn't be long."

The executive secretary straightened the button line of her white silk blouse as she entered her boss's private office. The shadow of her svelte shape was silhouetted against a wall-map by the emerging sun.

Thirtyish and poised, Mrs. Carruthers made light conversation, undoubtedly aware most visitors to the governor's office were somewhat anxious.

I didn't expect Jacobs to be alone when he entered the reception room. He wore a controlled grin as he bounced over to pump my hand and invite me into the privacy of his sumptuous office. The sweep of his arm directed me to a stuffed chair that was curiously lower than the dark swivel chair he occupied.

My near-contemporary spoke first. "We have a great mutual friend in Jack Clay, don't we?"

I agreed, elaborating to the point of repetition.

Governor Jacobs studied me, but it was not intense and apparently not meant to unnerve me.

Beginning with a lie, he said, "I don't like to meddle in local politics, but Jack Clay told me you'd make a fine mayor, so I promised to meet with you. The report of Mayor Baker's resignation is circulating."

Was using Marcella's title the governor's cue to address him formally? His boyish face and my aversion to titles made me decide not to call him anything unless the lack of doing so would appear too obvious.

"Yes, I believe it's true," I answered. "I am interested in replacing her, but I'm undecided on the best method of campaigning since the electorate will not choose her successor. I've never been involved in an intramural election where the same procedure is used to vote for a prospective officeholder as in picking a pavement contractor. I can only guess at the most effective strategy. After the speculation spread last night about Marcella quitting, Boss Kane from the Labor Temple said that a screening committee would meet soon with candidates. Democratic and Republican screening groups can be expected to follow shortly."

The governor wore a blue-black suit with pale stripes. A maroon tie with a wide knot fitted snugly against a white shirt with long collar points.

"You realize," Jacobs said comfortably, "that you should cultivate a close relationship with Kane and Tubby Stewart, the president of the aircraft workers' local. They are the two most powerful labor leaders in Burlington."

He mentioned the power of labor bosses, but not the Democratic party hierarchy.

I had waited for the opportune time to steer our discussion toward the issues and away from personalities, but the governor did it for me.

"I know a trifle about your background, Connor. What I don't know is where we stand on the issues, if there are any in Burlington."

"There are no real issues which could be bracketed into liberal or conservative matters," I said. "I suppose this usually is the case in city or county politics. There is one item, however, that needs some adversary scrutiny and that is the cable television franchise."

Governor Jacobs was on the edge of his high-backed chair. "Excuse me for interrupting, Connor, but I've heard payola is being distributed by cable TV lobbyists."

"How did it come up?" I asked without inflection

so as not to betray my skepticism. Political insiders hear plethoric rumors of collusion. I committed myself early to being a Thomas, giving scant attention to accusations until documentary evidence was proffered. Still, it was an eye-opener to hear the governor speak unguardedly to a virtual stranger.

"In addition to constitutional duties," he answered, "a governor must put out periodic fires, and decentralized listening posts are the surest means of finding flames while they're manageable. As you can imagine, my aides have antennae around the state."

The governor asked for my confidence and I gave it to him.

"Some respected persons came to me last evening. My chief assistant was present. They told of the sudden acquisition by four city council members of new cars and in two cases, pontoon boats. All the cars and boats allegedly came from Suburban Motors and Lakeside Marine. Both companies are divisions of Cableview, Incorporated, whose chief executive officer and largest stockholder is Albert Kelder, the most aggressive applicant for the cable TV franchise in Burlington. The invoices were said to have been routed through out-of-state factories and not through the local dealers."

The governor paused, as if to question something he had said.

"I'm not sure how this information reached my sources, but I believe it was through an employee of Lakeside Marine."

Another pause. He seemed to be in a quandary

regarding the wisdom of telling the story.

"This same Albert Kelder," he continued, "must want to lengthen his tentacles, as he made an appointment with me through my legislative liaison. I intended to ask him whether it is true that cars and boats have found their way into garages of council members in Burlington. That may be the best way to ward off an attempt to collude me."

I decided not to push for names of those involved, but I felt the governor should know of a related aspect. "If Sonny Wallace is one of the city council members who received a car or boat," I cautioned, "you may wish to be informed that Wallace and County Attorney Max Nabors are close friends."

As Governor Jacobs mulled my offering, I began to think that Wallace might be hearing from the state's chief executive before the day was out.

We were sounding like gossipers, so I moved the conversational fare to his inaugural address. "I favor your plan to convince manufacturers to locate factories in some of the state's more depressed cities."

"Thank you, Connor. My goal is to persuade smaller companies to do some of their production work in the lower central region of the state where the crop yield for several years has been unsatisfactory. In that way, farm women, youngsters and even the farmer himself could fall back on an outside income in case of crop failure. It should be attractive to management, too. Even with unionization, city wages would not have to be paid. The only requisite is that the smaller towns would have to have current rail service."

As the governor rang for coffee, he asked my pardon for perusing the first of the day's mail his secretary had brought him.

He glanced at each letter and went on. "Because the budgetary powers of this office were increased during the last legislative session, I have spent many days and evenings attempting to establish fiscal priorities. If you were in my position, with a greater flexibility but with no additional revenue, which expenditure would you pare and which would you augment?"

Being a member of the house of representatives, I knew last year's budget as well as the geographical borders of the district I represented. But he was not posing a fiscal question. By asking which expenditures I'd boost and which I'd deflate, he was finding out where my political heart lay. It was an ideological question.

"If I'm not mistaken, you're more interested in my heroines and heroes than in the budget."

His look told me I had read him correctly.

"My idols come in two categories. The professed religious who give their lives to God, the social workers, the nurses and those who volunteer spare hours to help the elderly and the poor; these are the people who live outside of self. Their names are seldom in the newspapers, but without them, our society would collapse."

Jacobs had no response.

"In the other category, and just as great, are the

factory workers and secretaries and black people who raise families on salaries that are sometimes as little as five per cent of their bosses' earnings. These are the ones who are threatened with layoffs, firings, piecework remuneration. They are called everything, including un-American, if they bargin for pension rights and greater benefits, while their superiors are paid in stock options and disproportionate salaries. These little people buy houses, keep marriages together and make efforts at being good parents on such low take-home pay, they're often forced to work two jobs. These are the people I would want to emulate."

Mrs. Carruthers knocked and entered with several messages. Jacobs and I both were silent until she started to leave after closing the drapes to shield us from the sun.

It was time to draw him out. "May I ask what types you esteem, Allard?" I wanted Sally Carruthers to hear me omit her boss's title. She hurried out of the office, glancing peripherally at me as she shut the door.

Ready with an answer and happy that I had asked, the governor said, "In a more nebulous way than yours, I admire the socially progressive activists operating in the political stable. They're usually ahead of their time and have the courage to withstand the scorn that's always evident until the public has accepted their reform ideas. This is the main reason I chose the Democratic party. It's constantly pressing for change in our society."

My probe into the governor's makeup didn't last

long: "Incidentally, Connor, what do you believe are the high points of the two major parties?"

"The Republican party," I said, "favors individual initiative, local control of government, responsible spending and other worthy objectives. But I joined the Democratic party because, historically, it has been the ombudsman for the immigrant, the laborer, the black, the farmer, and lately, the female. I am not very happy with the party right now, though. There are so many radicals espousing libertarian, anti-family goals, I expect some deep divisions at the next convention."

The governor sat more rigidly in his chair. "What do you think about health services?" he probed.

I wasn't sure where he was going with that question.

"We rank near the top in per capita doctors, nurses and hospitals," I said.

"What about family planning clinics?" he asked. "Would you have the state fund them?"

Now I understood his direction. He was pushing toward what he probably knew was the big difference we had, and I could not back away.

As slowly and deliberately as possible, I said, "If the clinics were under my control, I would lock their doors until equal time was given to natural methods of spacing children."

I wanted to close out the governor's thrust as firmly as I could and get on to his apparent ultimate purpose, to justify the killing of unborn children.

"Even if both artificial and natural methods

were available," he asked, "would you object to clinics using a post-conception type of birth control? I suppose you believe a human being exists at the time a woman conceives."

"You suppose correctly," I said, staring at him. "So do the geneticists at the university you and I both attended. They will tell you that at the moment of conception a child has genes that are unique in history."

Governor Jacobs tapped the fingers of his right hand on the surface of his desk. He was preparing to do battle and so was I.

"I won't argue with what the geneticists say, but I will speak of quality of life. It can be said legitimately that one life often is more important than another."

"You use the word 'legitimate'," I interrupted. "Which people can set themselves up as legitimate judges of who shall live and who shall die? Isn't that God's province? I think it's a little presumptuous for you to say a class of people—such as fetal children—does not have the right to life. The next thing you'll be saying is that blacks, retarded persons, convicts and maybe anyone not in power will be dispatched to the crematorium. This is the same quality of life of which Hitler spoke."

The governor was silent and livid. I continued: "If you doubt the completeness of the fetus when it is still in the embryonic state," I said, with hands outstretched, "a gynecologist can tell you that the unborn child has every internal organ it will ever have as an adult when it weighs only one-thirtieth of an once."

I finally was stopped. Governor Jacobs was shaking his head. "Hold it," he said, "I know of no good reason to be served in engaging in an extended discussion concerning our positions. I had hoped for certain reforms and I was gratified the supreme court acted. Your position is an honorable one, one which is obviously strongly held and one which springs from noble and humane ideals. Likewise, I regard my position as humane. It is a position others may well disagree with, but it is one arrived at only after careful reflection. I believe it is an honorable one."

As I had been told by Bert Miller, the governor's friend from high school, Allard Jacobs had not researched the topic of abortion, so he spoke in generalities and platitudes. Humane. Honorable. He didn't know the meaning of the words.

"Mr. Jacobs," I said firmly, unable to call him Allard or Governor, "if you think it is Democratic or liberal to approve of the killing of little babies in the womb, I have nothing more to say to you."

He was aghast.

I was not unmindful of the consequences of arguing with and finally insulting the governor at a time I was supposedly seeking his potent help. But I had made promises to myself and I wouldn't go back on my conviction that the right to life had deep American as well as Jewish and Christian roots.

I didn't shake his hand or say anything else to him. I merely stood and left his office as he looked pained and surprised. Why was he surprised when he forced and channeled the subject?

I walked rapidly to my car, disappointed and

upset. When the governor of a state could make statements such as I had just heard, and then expect a dignified response, I knew I was living in an animal society.

— ★ ★ ★ —

I drove out of Burlington through the Sioux Valley to the ghetto suburb of Edmondville, a few miles into Falvey County.

Just beyond the poorest section of town, a black priest, with the help of parishioners, had built a grotto to honor the Blessed Virgin Mary. It was a facsimile of Massabieille Cove near Lourdes in the French foothills of the Pyrenees, where the Lady of the Immaculate Conception had appeared to young Bernadette Soubirous over a century ago.

I felt more relaxed now, being away from the hum and problems of the city. I parked near the gate and walked a circuitous path to the shrouded statue of the Virgin, set unobtrusively behind and above naked rose bushes.

When I prayed to Mary, I asked that she intercede on behalf of the million or more unborn children who will die this year in the United States at the hands of quality-of-life advocates. I also implored the Lady to remember pro-life candidates all over the country who will encounter hostile endorsing committees.

This suburb was an appropriate place to pray for the conceived. I never had any doubts that blacks were the prime targets of the foundations that backed efforts to remove legal restrictions on abortion.

DECISION AT BURLINGTON

I closed my visit with a prayer for the diminutive colleen who chose two decades ago to marry another man. My Ann Marie.

III

Though it was only noontime, the driver of the car behind me alternated his low and high beam headlights as I entered downtown Burlington. Then, the lights flashed on and off. I couldn't tell if it was an unmarked police car, a friend or a maniac.

At the first intersection, I turned the corner and stopped. Maybe the driver would continue, I thought, trying to halt another driver.

Waving frantically, Jack Clay curbed his Mercedes sedan ahead of my hardtop. I stepped out and opened his passenger door and looked in. He was the last person I wanted to see right then. It wasn't a matter of procrastination, but I had to organize my explanation before reporting to Jack of my ruptured talk with Governor Jacobs. Regardless of what I said, however, Jack would be disappointed.

"I'm sorry, Jack, but my meeting with Allard went sour. All I can say is that I didn't plan it that way."

"I wasn't even thinking of that appointment," he said. "You can tell me later what happened. Right now, something strange is going on. Walter Manville just resigned from the city council, saying the governor had made him the first fulltime chairman of the Ecology Department over at the Capitol."

"Manville had been Mayor Baker's most vocal and experienced critic. City Hall insiders figured him to be waiting for Marcella's retirement at the scheduled end of her term before launching his long-dormant mayoral campaign."

"From what you've said," I remarked, "it doesn't seem all that strange for him to accept what eventually will mean a promotion. He's probably allowed to switch his pension rights under the agreement signed by the legislature and city council last year. I agree it's ironic he resigned when rumors spread through downtown about the possibility that Marcella might not finish her term. But maybe Manville is sick of city government and wants a change. He's been a councilman for nine and one-half years."

"All that makes sense," Jack agreed, "but Manville has no outside income and the funding provided at the last legislative session for the Ecology Department will not start until five months from now. You know that, of course, having been on the committee that conducted the hearings."

"Another funny thing is that Manville always jousted with the ecologists who came before the city council. I suppose this appointment can be looked upon as a politician in search of security. Yet, I don't know..." he trailed off.

With Baker and Manville resigning, there were only seven council members remaining; or eight, if Manville's vacancy were filled before a new mayor was elected. The great power expressed by only seven or eight people voting for the next leader of government in this large, highly industrialized city was frightening.

"Only a few people will decide your immediate future," Jack said, "so you may be dunned by council members in exchanged for their votes, or by power blocs which promise council votes. Wouldn't it be wise for you to have stock answers ready for any possible bribe attempts? Just so no one can misinterpret your positions?"

"Yes, I suppose so. I used to be shocked when I'd hear a veteran activist repeat a demand made by someone in a position of strength. But my naivete is gone now. I think I'd have the right answers."

I returned to my car, having agreed to meet Jack at City Hall to peruse the city charter section dealing with council resignations. As president of the body, the mayor would be included in the same section as that which covered city council members.

While waiting in the municipal arcade for Jack to arrive, I purchased the first evening edition of the Burlington *Courier*. Not unexpectedly, the headline read, "MAYOR BAKER TO RESIGN?" The accompanying article was brief, stating that Marcella would make an announcement in the next week. Jack entered the building through the main entrance, hurrying over to where I was leaning against the newspaper dispenser.

Another article on the front page told of Walter Manville's resignation from the city council for the more lucrative Ecology job.

I handed the paper to Jack. He read the stories without comment or a change of expression. I thought Jack also might be convinced that more was involved with Manville than the state appointment by Governor Jacobs.

The concrete building housing most city and county offices had been constructed by the Works Progress Administration during the depression of the 1930s. Though relatively modern, its elevators still were not automatic. Standing next to their cages were four of the twelve operators. As Jack and I approached, the one nearest us said in a hushed aside, "That's Mullaney on the right. He's going to be a candidate." Those standing by turned toward us and gawked. I was flabbergasted.

We alighted from the elevator at the seventh floor and walked down a corridor lined with highly polished black marble to the city attorney's office.

Inside were staggered secretarial desks which separated the front counter from a law library and private offices. No one appeared to be working. Stenographic employees were standing and conversing with two senior prosecutors.

Noticing me, one of the attorneys stopped his exchange abruptly and waved a printed sheet, saying, "I think this is what you want to see, Mr. Mullaney." It was the city charter provision on special elections. Jack and I laughed at the matter of fact approach.

The section of the city charter noted, "In the event of the mayor's resignation or removal from office before the end of term, an intramural election will be held by remaining city council members to select a successor. To be eligible, one must be at least eighteen years of age, a registered voter, and a six months' resident of the City of Burlington. No member of the city council shall be eligible for the vacated seat of the mayor."

Jack and I gave each other knowing looks. Walter Manville had heard unimpeachable sources tell of Mayor Baker's planned resignation and he quit before her so that he could claim he was not a council member when she resigned. Very clever. Now we knew there were at least two candidates for the vacancy.

We dropped into Marcella Baker's suite of offices to see if we were correct. The mayor read the section of the charter and then the newspaper articles and she agreed it appeared Manville would be a candidate for mayor.

Did all of this mean Manville lined up favorable votes for himself before resigning? He was a veteran council member, the type who never took an irretrievable public step without first testing his strength.

The mayor waited while Clay and I phoned Bart Countryman. Jack briefed him while Marcella and I listened.

"My initial reaction," Bart said, "is that Manville knowingly preempted Marcella in order to run for mayor. I can't see him leaving without the votes needed to bring him back into the mayor's office. Then again, it's a maverick council. Even the labor mouthpieces occasionally think independently."

Bart accepted the task of calling some of the Democratic leaders and all of the city council members, pointedly asking the latter if Manville had their votes.

Before leaving, Jack and I urged Marcella not to accelerate her termination timetable out of fear others on the city council would precede her in quitting in order to be candidates. At this juncture, remaining in office for several weeks would aid me by preventing the council from making a backroom replacement before any endorsing bodies convened.

Marcella walked us to the door of her office suite. "Over at the capitol, Connor," she said, "you may not be conscious of the power of the aircraft workers' union. It's too bad that the factory isn't in your legislative district. Then you'd have had past support from them and more clout at the Labor Temple. How well do they know you, over and above your dealings with their lobbyists?"

"They certainly are aware of my support for and sponsorship of bills relating to strengthening Labor's hand. I don't like closed shops because of the non-union man's loss of freedom of choice, even though I'm versed in the need for inseparability in negotiations. The aircraft people know this about me. I've often expected an argument from them over the closed shop, but it never has happened."

As we parted, Marcella asked Jack Clay to fill me in on Walter Manville's association with Al Kelder.

For privacy and time to confer, Jack and I took the stairway down to the street. I told him of Kelder pestering the governor's aide for an appointment, and Jack recounted Manville's bold support of Kelder's company as the best cable TV franchisee for Burlington. That could pinpoint Manville as the council member who set up the payola from Suburban Motors and Lakeside Marine.

When we reached the street arcade, Jack called Bart Countryman again from a public telephone. Cupping his hand over the telephone, Jack said, "So far, Bart's getting denials from the council. They all claim Manville did not ask for their votes and if he had, they wouldn't have guaranteed anything. Sonny Wallace said a commitment to vote for someone would be an improper request by the would-be candidate and a questionable promise by the city council member.

At the last state Democratic convention, Wallace didn't think it was questionable or improper to press for delegate commitments. But he would say that that was not analogous.

IV

Forcing myself to attend the regular monthly meeting of the ninety-sixth district Democratic club, whose umbrella covered one senate and three house districts, including mine, I found it even more difficult to stay for its entirety. When a Eurocommunist propaganda movie short—billed as a documentary—was shown to the packed hall, most of those in attendance cheered at the end.

As I started to leave without asking for the club's endorsement, Lieutenant Governor Meredith Calvin burst into the room and pressed up to the podium. I stayed and heard him orate sanctimoniously about the state having a duty to rent billboards to publicize the location of abortion clinics. Very few in the assemblage saw me. It was just as well.

When I slipped out to the parking lot, a group of women were weeping and consoling each other. They were party regulars. I recognized most of them. They saw me coming and one of the women wiped her eyes and related to me in a quiet way how Mary Candless, a young and tireless party executive, had died suddenly after a brief respiratory illness. The housewife had been at various times a county chairwoman, vice-chairperson of the state party machinery and national committeewoman.

Although saddened by her death, of relevance

to me was her chairwomanship of the Burlington Democratic screening committee, that which candidates appeared before to seek endorsements.

The party bylaws stated that vacating chairpersons would be succeeded by their assistants, so I assumed Archibald Smythe would head the screening committee.

I made a mental note to find some background on Smythe, particularly the faction to which he belonged within the party.

— ★ ★ ★ —

Things were unfolding quickly, so I called the Democratic chairman of Burlington's congressional district, Ulric Anderson, at a huge contracting firm which did over fifty per cent of its business with different governmental bodies. I was unable to get a hint of his job or department identity because he had a direct dial number and answered the phone himself.

"Ulric, this is Connor Mullaney. I'm interested in succeeding Mayor Baker if she resigns and I'm calling for your support. Can we meet for lunch?" It was the most unimaginative opening statement I could have made.

There was silence at the other end of the line, leaving me with little doubt as to how the conversation would conclude.

Finally, Anderson said icily, "Are you the same Connor Mullaney who did not respect the governor's view of the right to terminate a pregnancy?"

"Did you expect parlor manners," I replied, "when our state's chief executive said he thinks feticide is humane? Don't I have a right to express my opinion?"

My adrenalin was at work. Would he hang up if I told him I was proud then and I was still proud I let the governor have it? I had spoken the way I did to Allard Jacobs with full awareness it would probably damage me when I sought other endorsements.

I tried not to raise my voice. My audience was intent on misquoting me.

Anderson spoke with deliberation: "I just wanted to know if I had the right man."

I was angry. "What does that mean, Ulric?"

"Oh, nothing," he said, "but now I'm sure I have the right man."

I pressed him. "What didn't you like about my visit with the governor?"

"Well, I thought it was indiscreet...and of poor judgement," the district chairman said redundantly.

"By the way, Ulric, what's your stand on abortion?"

The local Democratic leader, who declaimed regularly about shepherding the helpless, told me what he favored doing with the classically helpless: "I approve of the right to remove the product of conception."

"Do you think the manner in which I reacted with the governor would not have seemed indiscreet if you opposed abortion?"

No, that had nothing to do with it. Of course.

This was an official of a political party which championed controversy as the most acceptable avenue to take in the quest for truth; a party in which factional fights were commonplace and in which the

DECISION AT BURLINGTON

right to freedom of speech was held to be nearly sacred.

I tried to analyze Anderson's motives as I hung up. As a party executive, he worked many evenings and weekends on political matters, visiting state senate district meetings to report the latest news from the congressional district office.

Last year, a non-election year, he seemed to have been at his political office more than not, and during the work week. What type of agreement did he have with his employer, I wondered, when he could slip into city council meetings almost every day? I didn't have to ask the question, though. His company urged its employees to be active in all strata of politics, making them inexpensive and sometimes unwitting lobbyists. For any employee who ran for the state legislature, the company managed to divert corporate funds to a foreign back account. This was a company practice long before the process came to be known as laundering money.

When one was in politics for awhile, he questioned the purpose of nearly everyone who remained active after the initial euphoria faded. The young party members usually were without self-ambition. As they married and became involved in their jobs and families, their interest dwindled away. Those intent on holding office, party or public, stayed with the party through all the long-winded speeches, the boring meetings, the raffles, the partisan nonsense, and worst, the omnipresent superficiality. Ulric Anderson had been active for a goodly period, but I didn't know his motivation.

DECISION AT BURLINGTON

I went directly to the Democratic party office to seek out Anderson's chief aide, Bill Sailor. As I leafed through campaign propaganda, Sailor told me of some new senate district chairpersons. He also spoke of ambition in the party, so I brought up the question of Ulric's ultimate goal.

"He would accept a draft for the mayoral opening," Sailor said forthrightly, answering the question of motivation.

The fundraiser and executive assistant invited me to a quiet bar next door to the Democratic headquarters for a beer. A former reporter, Sailor best could be described as a civil liberties' Democrat. That was the class of party members former United States Senator Richard Carter had brought to the fore. Most of his backers were not acquainted with nor cared about the dreams and problems of the labor wing of the party.

Sailor, a mustachioed chainsmoker, sat on a bar stool with one foot atop an adjacent stool. I walked around to the other side and mounted a soft leather perch.

We talked amiably before I opened up the subject we both had retired to the bar to discuss: "I am upset that Ulric Anderson doesn't think I have a right to freedom of expression with the governor. Then I hear from you that Ulric is a closet candidate for mayor. I'm beginning to think he's a hypocrite."

Sailor was letting me make my point without interrupting. He had always been a gentleman with me, but this time I believed his silence was due to not having a ready answer.

He chose his words carefully. "It was not so much your abruptness with the governor, but the extent of your involvement in the pro-life movement."

I wasn't certain that I heard him correctly. "Do you mean," I asked, "that a person should only be half-committed to something be believes in?"

"Well, if you hadn't organized that protest at the capitol...it was that day Ulric disavowed his earlier interest in your party future. You know, Connor, I simply can't agree with your position that abortion is murder."

Sailor said it kindly.

"You're too involved," he continued. "You'd be divisive in the party."

"You know what your faction needs," I said, "is a candidate who takes no firm stands, holds nothing inviolate, and believes only in furthering himself politically. Then he could rationalize any principle. A person with a calculating mentality, shaping his position to accommodate the prize. The end justifying the means. That's situation ethics and I think it stinks."

The conversation drifted to another subject, but I got that for which I had come. The words echoed in my ears: "...the extent of your involvement."

V

In the wake of the hatchet job Ulric Anderson performed on me, I started phoning city council members rather than spending any more time contacting persons on the periphery of power.

I couldn't get through to the Commissioner of Schools, Sonny Wallace. In Burlington, city council members were called commissioners, because, under the commission form of government, they were the administrative heads of departments in addition to being city legislators.

Each time I'd give my name, Wallace's secretary asked if it was something the deputy commissioner could handle.

Sam Talbot, Commissioner of Police, was cordial and humorous, saying there were so many candidates, he was going to start charging for the phone calls. Talbot said he had no favorite. That was encouraging, even though he didn't say he would promote my candidacy.

Fire Commissioner Constance Wetherby inquired, "Have you met with Hayden?"

I informed her I had not as yet contacted Ellsworth M. Hayden, Commissioner of Finance.

That did not pacify Commissioner Wetherby. "He's not fit to be a member of the city council," she said in a pique.

I didn't know what Hayden's fitness had to do with me. I merely listened while she unleashed her attack.

Mrs. Wetherby emphasized she didn't have a commitment to any candidate yet, with stress on the adverb.

After an article in the morning *Courier* regarding my entrance into the race, several people stopped me on the street. One of them was Walter Manville, the man responsible for the city council vacancy.

"Welcome to the battle," he said, thereby confirming his own candidacy. "My problem is finding a job for my deputy commissioner. I imagine you're aware that the deputy's out of a job when the commissioner resigns."

That was Walter's way of putting down a politician from another legislative body, telling him the obvious. It was like explaining the American League's designated hitter rule to a National Leaguer.

Former Commissioner Manville's show of concern for his now unemployed deputy commissioner, Clark Mathews, was not as unselfish as he let on. The filling of Manville's seat would follow the same intramural election pattern as with the mayor. I imagined the elections would be held in the same chronological order of the vacancies. Therefore, if Manville could get Mathews elected to the council vacancy, he could be assured a crucial vote for mayor, because Mathews already would have been seated. Then there would be eight council members voting for the new mayor.

Commissioner of Administration Bert Peterson and George Zachman, Commissioner of Parks, Recreation and Stadia, listened to my pitch. The former was cool, the latter friendly. These were the two Republicans and representatives of downtown businessmen. They were seen often in huddles with vice-presidents of the larger banks, hotels and department stores, who had almost daily needs for minor ordinance changes. More freed traffic lanes. A pedestrian stoplight in mid-block. The cleaning of streets only in the middle of the night. More transit shelters. The needs were constant. So was the flow of campaign funds to Peterson and Zachman.

I didn't call Ellsworth Hayden. I couldn't bring myself to do it. Because of the way he bullied people, his vote could be the most important at this time. But I didn't respect him and in fact I was apprehensive about calling him for fear he would propose something illegal.

Public Works' Commissioner Winona Smith was reported out of town.

— ★ ★ ★ —

Almost immediately after starting his telephone work on my behalf, Bart Countryman encountered flak. Ninety-sixth House district chairwoman Darcy Braun's feelings were hurt because I didn't ask for her imprimatur. It was an oversight on my part. The thought to call her simply had not occurred to me, probably because I only was a sometime member of the district club. It wasn't pragmatic of me, but I was less comfortable with the bolsheviks controlling the group than with some of the most myopic Republicans in town.

Being close to Ulric Anderson, Darcy would be further upset with me after she found out the result of my telephone conversation with Anderson. She could impede my candidacy with fellow district chairpersons and perhaps she would do just that.

When Countryman bored in on Darcy to support me, she told him I was elected a delegate to the national convention six years ago, but didn't go. "It might have been forgotten," she had said, "but the alternate delegate made a fool of himself. There was some talk that Republicans convinced Mullaney not to go."

Countryman said he slapped the innuendo by demanding: "What's that supposed to mean, Darcy? If you're accusing him of some impropriety, be explicit. Don't sneak around the corner."

Darcy told him she didn't have anything concrete, so Bart warned her that she'd better bury her allusions unless she wanted to look at a lawsuit.

After retelling their conversation, Countryman asked me, "Exactly why did you decline going to the national convention?"

"I could say the convention conflicted with a business trip and I'd be accurate, but the underlying reason was that I heard belatedly that the left-wingers intended to wreck it. I wanted no part of something intentionally counterproductive. I wasn't sure I did the right thing until I saw a picture of the riot on television."

With mocking understatement, Bart said, laughing, "That sounds like an exercise of good judgement and legitimate prerogative."

I was perturbed. If Bart had not roughhoused Darcy, her intimation may have proliferated into an allegation of wrongdoing.

Her attempt to discredit me was not atypical in the murky world of politics, where the most efficacious method of brightening one's star was to step on someone else. But here was a young woman I really didn't know well and to whom I had paid little attention. . .and she was attacking me!

I was beginning to think Countryman was the most apt candidate. His challenge of Darcy was well done.

After trying for two days, I reached former two-term mayor Vin Norris, the immediate predecessor of Mayor Baker.

"Ulric Anderson turned his howitzer on me, Vin, but I cannot change my pro-life position for anyone."

Quickly, Vin urged, "Don't ever change. I'll make some calls around town and see what I can do."

After a frustrating day, I was buoyed by the offer of help from this still powerful political figure.

Bart Countryman and Jack Clay were impressed even more. "If Vin supports your candidacy," Jack said, "you have to be regarded as a strong contender."

This helped me realize my decision to limit contacts to city council members was a mistake. Persons such as Vin Norris and those few party and labor leaders whom I respected might not be able to promise votes, but their magnetism with some of the commissioners had to be a factor. The council certainly was not impenetrable.

－－ ★　★　★ －

Marcella Baker had left an urgent call at my answering service. When I reached her, she said one of her family's businesses was very close to receivership. The family banker notified her that her husband had tried to secure a loan while drunk. Marcella didn't have to tell me the rest. She would have to resign immediately.

Mayor Baker had called the Republican and Democratic chairpersons and the head of the Labor Temple to let them be ready to screen candidates.

I could see that the screening would be a disorganized mess, what with the council and mayoral screening going on at the same time, and the seating of the mayor being held up for the selection of the new Commissioner of Utilities.

I arranged a hurried conference at the Chaix-Gordon Hotel with Countryman, Clay, Norris and Marcella, if she could make it.

Clay and I met as the rush hour started. The hotelier gave us an unobtrusive dining room near the lobby. He was instructed to exclude everyone except Marcella and Bart.

Jack had the predictable news that Labor Temple screening would commence tomorrow. He couldn't get any information about Democratic and Republican screening schedules, if there were any at this point.

Mayor Baker and Bart Countryman arrived as

Jack and I considered the idea of ignoring all screening and endorsement gatherings. That was not because we had any surety Vada Griffin would be treated as labor's best friend and unquestioned endorsee. It rather was a matter of knowing we would reach an impasse with one of the endorsing groups over the rights of unborn children.

Jack phoned a public stenographer and dictated a press release, spelling out my unyielding position on abortion.

We spent the next two hours listening to Marcella discuss every major item in the four hundred twenty million dollar budget. Then we had an hour-long question period, with Marcella supplying the answers. After she left, Jack and Bart shook their heads in awe of her brilliance and photographic memory. I was not suprised. In her three terms, I could say that I learned from her every time we conferred.

For all the campaigns of which Bart had been an integral part, I couldn't understand why he never assisted his Democratic sister. If he was unimpressed with her in the past, I thought she had made a believer of him today.

VI

On a visit to the district Democratic headquarters, I met again with fundraiser Bill Sailor. He reported that party leaders did not want to elevate Deputy Commissioner Clark Mathews to the vacant council position, as they did not consider him a viable candidate for next fall's at-large election.

"After all," Sailor quoted the party hierarchy as saying, "Mathews can always go back to the parks' department job he held before becoming a deputy."

It may have been prudent thinking, but I didn't like it because it would break the unwritten rule of a deputy being named to his chief's vacancy.

I, the gadfly, drove directly to City Hall after leaving Sailor and sought Clark Mathews in the council chamber. I told him exactly what I had heard. I knew it would cause him pain, but it was best, I concluded, that he heard what the powers were planning.

The deputy commissioner grimaced, making a high-pitched complaint: "Why don't they ask Mathews what he thinks is best for himself? Doesn't it matter that I do not want to return to the parks' department?"

I left the building and leaving my car in the City Hall lot, I took a cab to the Labor Temple where integrated council and mayoral screening was ready to begin. Entering the building through the side door, I bypassed the single, eternally slow elevator and went up the stairway. As I climbed two steps at a time, I nearly bumped into Tubby Stewart, head of the powerful aircraft workers' union and a man who had refused to make an appointment with me. I entertained no hope of gaining his support and I was not sure why. With a nod to Stewart, I continued upward.

Three well-known candidates were seated on folding chairs outside the interviewing room when I arrived. Onetime state legislator Gus Kegler was there. A neat dresser, he did not look the part of a scrap metal dealer.

In a muffled conversation with Phil Drake, emeritus head of the Labor Temple, was Labor's favorite son, Vada Griffin.

Standing against a wall with cigarette in hand was city auditor Earl Sanford, soon to be one of the job casualties of the city-county merger.

A few lesser known hopefuls ascended the steps as Griffin received the first call to be screened. Those of us remaining in the hallway made small talk. When my turn came, I was dismayed to find only nine persons, including one woman, in the screening room. There were one hundred and sixty-seven unions in the Temple membership. Either many proxy votes were being cast or the minds of the selection committee had already been made up. Even so, I felt comfortable in the dingy room where the furniture was unintentional King Arthur.

I began my presentation by telling those present

of my belief in the need for collective bargaining and of my hope that more blacks and chicanos would be enrolled in unions. Stares. I peered inquiringly at Boss Kane, executive secretary of the Labor Temple and business agent for the business agents. He shot back an approving smile.

Labor patriarch Phil Drake interrupted me, asking my opinion of compulsory arbitration. My answer was not to his liking, so he graced the sparse assemblage with one of his doctrinaire monologues. I suspected that Drake had determined my answer would be wrong before it was stated.

Soon the screening was over. Labor had listened to my case; its obligation to me had ceased; democracy had been served.

I left the interviewing room and spotted Clark Mathews. Maybe my disclosure to him about party plans to dump him put some spunk into his city council candidacy. I took him aside and repeated the questions I had been asked. It was possible mayoral questions would not be posed to those auditioning for the council, but Mathews at least could have recognized the gesture.

As I walked slowly down the wooden steps to the street, I heard the clump-clump of heavy boots.

"Hey, Mullaney," a throaty male called casually, belying the haste of his approach.

When he moved closer, I was able to recognize Ralph Holden, business agent for several railroad unions, excepting the dining car workers. Even with our proximity, I was unable to interpret his expression. But I knew he had a point to make and it would be of one extreme or the other; to offer help from his unions or to take issue with something I had said in the screening room.

Ralph had risen steadily through the union ranks with an unbeatable system. He used criminal evidence for his strength. One man who had sold items stolen from boxcars became—by blackmail—an organizer for Ralph the stoolie, rounding up votes from rail workers for the annual business agent election.

A trainee conductor had had his schooling program shortened even before Ralph gained power. The conductor paid for the influence by poormouthing the then business agent, thereby speeding Ralph's takeover of the job.

Ralph once had witnessed two brakemen engaging in horseplay shortly before an eleven-car train derailed and overturned. Again by blackmail, the men became his informers, and when necessary, strongarm goons against the anti-Holden cliques that sprung up occasionally in the various unions for which Ralph was the chief business agent.

Ralph always kept notes and managed to have witnesses on hand for particularly sticky matters that were especially troublesome to his union men.

And so it went. He built up a favors' list that propelled him into control of the prosperous rail unions. That control was sustained by the frequent raises and increased fringe benefits his union members enjoyed.

So successful was this business agent that he contracted a disease common to many executives: He thought he was never wrong. This caused him to rule with no advisors, no committees and no procedural standards.

"You know everything, don't you?" Ralph Holden sputtered. "What right do you have, telling me I don't have enough blacks and chicanos in my unions? It's not my fault they can't pay the initiation fee!"

"But why is two hundred fifty of the three hundred dollar fee returned to whites but not to those whose skin is slightly darker?" I asked.

With that, he lunged at me with both fists flying. I pushed him to the ground and forced his forearm up his back nearly to his shoulder. Boss Kane and Phil Drake came running toward us, grabbing and admonishing the head of fifty-four hundred rail workers. I caught a cab back to City Hall where I picked up my car.

— ★ ★ ★ —

When I arrived home, I calmed myself with a strong bourbon on the rocks before calling Vin Norris at the Greeley Publishing Company, where he said he'd be going over a backlog of orders.

"Gosh, did I run into a buzz-saw when I called Ulric Anderson on your behalf," he said. "But I'm getting some good responses, too," he added quickly.

Norris had not lost his enthusiasm. He wanted me to check back with him after he had a chance to contact some of the key people on the Democratic central committee.

Following the first article that appeared with the speculation of Marcella's resignation, *Courier* editorialist Barry Siler stated emphatically to me that his newspaper was not going to endorse a candidate for mayor, primarily because it was not an at-large election, and the public might think the paper's influence was too great on the few persons making the decision.

In the afternoon's edition, though, twenty-four hours after Siler confided the non-endorsement to me, the *Courier* endorsed bureaucrat and independent Gordon Mallory for mayor. (In Burlington, some Republicans called themselves Independents.) I knew the editorial staff labeled Mallory mediocre at best, so the endorsement had to be printed at the behest of the Republican publisher. At least, I could be happy that the paper's endorsee was not Walter Manville. I spent the evening on the phone. The next morning I drove to City Hall to see what was developing in the council.

With Constance Wetherby on business in Washington, D.C., and Ellsworth Hayden on an unexplained absence, Commissioner Sonny Wallace introduced his proposed cable television ordinance. It was difficult for me to tell whether it favored franchise hopeful Al Kelder.

Commissioners Wetherby and Hayden seldom were away from the city for more than a day or two, so they could be expected to assist or oppose the next step for this bi-partisan monster: the preparation of an eligibility list for cable companies.

The day hurried by as I tried to prime myself for the evening grilling to be conducted by the Democratic screening committee.

— ★ ★ ★ —

As I drove down the elegant Capitol Boulevard to

the mansion of longtime Democrat Jimmy Hughes, I felt like a masochist.

Vada Griffin was to appear at seven o'clock and I was scheduled to make my presentation before the screening committee at seven-thirty. One-half hour didn't seem long enough for mayoral spielers.

Noticing Griffin and two other men standing on the open porch of the five story redstone showplace, I surmised that Democratic congressional district chairman Ulric Anderson was verbose in giving his charge to the committee. He would present five points to be considered in selecting the most desirable candidate: 1. the ability to gain at least five of the eight votes needed to win the seat; 2. electability in next fall's at-large election; 3. the chance of getting the Labor Temple's support; 4. belief in the *principles* of the Democratic party; and 5. the cerebral wherewithal to do the job.

I made light conversation with Griffin and Hughes, the host. The former was positive that Deputy Mathews would be named a full commissioner tomorrow morning in an unpublicized intramural vote in the city council.

Even though the cocky Griffin was thought of as a dullard, he had perfected elementary techniques to keep reporters, opponents and other detractors off balance. Instead of changing a subject and thereby inviting a more probing question, he deviated slightly from core points with branched, innocuous answers. Then he had a supporter direct a complimentary question to him. He always had the supporter present to protect his flank.

If he was really in a corner, he used frowns and sarcasm and huff and puff to divert attention from his oblique responses. Not original, but effective.

Shortly after Griffin was summoned by executive assistant Bill Sailor to start the questioning, Sailor surprised us by reappearing on the porch. Answering our startled looks, he said, "I can't stand Vada Griffin."

As I paced the stone floor of the huge, half-moon porch, the sun was setting on a pleasant spring day. Many thoughts gamboled through my mind. Would I be asked about revenue and general obligation bonds? Race and labor problems? Philosophical beliefs?

Being only an average extemporizer, I knew someone would cause me to stutter on an issue. My only real concern, though, was to be certain I didn't compromise anything I believed in.

As I paced about I carried on an engrossing conversation with Hughes' bearded son. Vada Griffin came out of the screening room pale and quiet. He left immediately.

I was directed into the fireplace room where a twenty-foot long oval table and its chairs were the only pieces of furniture. The first person I recognized was Darcy Braun, the woman who had declared to Bart Countryman: "Mullaney doesn't have a chance." The law student seemed to prefer the verdict before the trial.

My friend, David Shapiro, was at my right elbow. Next to him was Candy Durwood, a physician-housewife who ran—with party endorsement—

two unsuccessful campaigns for the city council. So far, three civil libertarians, with Braun, Shapiro and Durwood. Sailor, Anderson and District Chairwoman Geri Zanders were there. The latter two would have no votes, but their impact would be felt, certainly.

Two channel-vision radicals, Bobbi Pinson and Nathaniel St. George, were supposed to be present.

Ms. Pinson unquestionably was the pubescent, denim-clad tigress sitting on my left at the broadest part of the oval table. Her reputed goal was to have federally funded abortionists making weekly visits to each of Burlington's high schools. Truly, the enemy was before me!

The man I picked to be St. George showed the striking incongruity of early middle-aged plumpness and shoulder-length hair. A full professor at Metropole College, a hotbed for the far left, he took a seat next to Candy Durwood. His goal was said to be the nationalization of Burlington's industry.

Chairman Archibald Smythe was a young man unknown to me. I had heard his clipped confidence at party gatherings, but I didn't know how he leaned politically; that is, within the Democratic party. But my guess was that his pattern included ecology, an ignorance of labor's needs, pro-death in the womb but anti-death in the world's trouble spots, an unfamiliarity with Burlington's ghetto conditions because of an aristocratic upbringing, and finally, down deep, an earnest belief he someday would grace the governor's mansion.

DECISION AT BURLINGTON

The assistant chairman of the screening committee was Carleton Majors, scion of a family with substantial bank holdings. My classmate in college, Majors now was a vice-president of the First National Bank of Burlington. He was admired in local Democratic circles as an establishment executive whose concern for the masses was not abandoned as he climbed the corporate mountain. A man ordained to be a Good Shepherd for the lowly serfs of his province.

When Carleton and I were at the state university one generation ago, he once asked for an introduction to my girlfriend. Dutifully, I made the exchange of names. The following morning, my lady was awakened by a phone call from Carleton. She refused his request for a date then and four or five other times in subsequent weeks. During this period, when I saw him on campus, he played the part of the innocent buddy, wanting to converse about every extraneous thing.

Now the quisling wielded power on a committee sitting in judgement of my political credentials. Would he recall the college days' incident and try to seek some distorted revenge?

I carried with me into the screening room a document which explained Carleton's role as a double agent on the committee. I had had a disagreement with myself this afternoon over the document, which was a copy of a letter presented to me by a good friend from the First National Bank, one who was tired of contributing to conservative causes through arm-twisting. It had been the bank's policy

51

to assess in strong terms a substantial amount of money that management personnel had to contribute to the bank's political committee. Then the monies were given to the campaigns of various local and national conservative candidates without the giver having any control over the distribution. By contributing to the committee and not directly to the bank, a circumvention was made of the state Corrupt Practices Act, which prohibited corporations and banks from making material contributions to candidates for municipal and state offices.

I held a confidential, photocopied letter in my coat pocket from the bank's board chairman to Carlton, a onetime domestic snitch for the CIA, asking him to penetrate the Democratic screening meetings for a two-fold purpose: 1. to find any candidates acceptable to the conservative cause, so that the bank group could contribute to those persons' campaigns; and 2. to pick up strategy secrets and evidence of legal violations, returning the information to the bank, which would turn it over to the Republican party.

I didn't have a copy of Carleton's reply to the board chairman, if there was an answer, nor did I know whether there was sequential correspondence from the chairman. But I thought Carleton's presence at the screening spoke as his reply.

The reason I had an inward disagreement had to do with the moral correctness of holding the letter for defense in case Carleton attacked me. I decided I'd have to be personally affronted before I'd disclose the contents; although I would be morally obliged to do so after the election to expose the duplicity of both Carleton and the board chairman.

Almost before I could identify his face, I detected the plumage of Carleton Majors: blue, buckled shoes, fire red slacks, white belt, navy blue blazer, white on white silk shirt, red and white polka dot bow tie and a black toupee with a schoolboy hairline. If it was attention he was courting, he was successful. Six screeners encircled him as Chairman Smythe beseeched everyone to sit down.

Half-filled ash trays and note pads were positioned in front of each member of the committee.

Carleton sat across from Bobbi Pinson. Next to him was Sam Arnold, group insurance salesman and Jaycee extraordinaire, having been named recently as one of the ten outstanding young men in the state. Presumably, Sam was honored for bringing in more premium dollars than all other salespersons in his company this past year. A rising community pillar whose every day was spent in concern for those he caused to be underwritten.

Sam had been warned early in his professional career to exercise caution in expressing his opinions in the presence of corporate prospects. And since no one ever could say that potential clients were out of range, his speech always was tempered with the knowledge that he might alienate some poor souls who otherwise could have been protected by his company. Sam was philosophical about it. "Why take money out of the hands of possible widows?" he had been known to ask.

The message from the bottom of the ashtrays

shone through prismed glass: "For everything from group insurance to coffee chattin', give ol' Sam Arnold a call at 899-5329. He's a square shooter and he has a policy to fit your company's needs."

Sam could be expected to compliment the candidate and thank the committee before submitting the query: "What are your thoughts about the adequacy of the city employees' insurance and pension plans?"

To Sam's right was Allison Reynolds, a junior leaguer whose plutocratic position was somewhere in the expanse that separated the nouveau riche from the town's lone centimillionaire.

With her background, Allison certainly would not be defending increased welfare benefits, but I couldn't guess how she'd react on other issues. I did know, however, that it was best to be on the same side as Allison, for she was unrelenting with anyone who collided with her most dedicated concerns.

Always groomed to perfection, Allison perhaps was the most beautiful woman in Burlington. With deep-set pale blue eyes, a finely chiseled nose and a firm jaw, the slender housewife's honey blond tresses curled under her ears and above a starched pilgrim collar. Her white blouse was complemented by a middle blue flared skirt.

I had checked the city directory for the livelihood of the committee members. Of the twenty-six listed, I found only four that could be identified as being from organized labor. It made me nervous. Impressing country club liberals with the importance of negotiating as a unit was not going to win the group's laurel.

As I made my introductory remarks, congressional district chairman Ulric Anderson's eyes were fixed on the ceiling.

"There are two reasons some of you can support my candidacy, and then some may not support me for the same reasons. First, in next fall's general election, as well as in this upcoming contest, I will disclose the source and amount of every contributor to my campaign. I'll do this weekly. Second, I'm told I am too conservative. On that point, I can say I became a liberal because collective bargaining and strong unions with honest, fearless business agents will be needed as long as there are economic inequities."

"Another reason I am a liberal has to do with blacks, Chicanos and Indians. Countless civil rights' laws have been enacted since 1954, yet there are relatively few minority persons in positions of civic or industrial responsibility. This is a city of one and one-half million people, with a black population of twenty-nine percent. Now I don't excuse crime for any reason, but for all those sitting back and accusing blacks of causing a disproportionate share of Burlington's crime, I say, expand on the good will the white population has shown. Let the blacks be skilled building tradesmen, sales managers, legal secretaries, school superintendents. Treat them as the American citizens they are. Incidently, the four hundred fifty thousand blacks in Burlington voted eighty-three percent Democratic in the last election. May I ask why this twenty-six person Democratic committee has only two blacks?"

No one said anything, so I went on. "The thrust of my message tonight is that I believe the talented, the affluent and those with strengths of mind and emotion have a great responsibility to help those with very little in the way of money, skills and hope. In a simple explanation, this is why I am a Democrat."

"Because the exodus to the suburbs is increasing steadily, our change from city to county government, with a broadening tax base, is coming at the most helpful time. Although the demand for services is progressively greater, I do not have bad news to report about the Burlington ledger book. Mayor Baker may have been the best mayor this city ever had. If I am elected to succeed her, I'll be seeking her advice on fiscal and other matters."

"We only have a half hour so it's probably best that I ask now for questions."

Chairman Smythe was first: "In what ways are you conservative?"

I started to answer, "Well, first, I'll tell you..."

Smythe startled me, snapping, "Just answer the question!"

At that point, David Shapiro came to my rescue. "Can't we ask specific liberal or conservative questions," he pleaded.

There was a pause, so I began as best I could. "I am a conservative in the intangible areas." I was stalling to shape my presentation. "The breakdown in the family structure is nearly epidemic. Abortion and general permissiveness are two manifestations of eroding family discipline."

In addition to the chairman, I had angered one other man. He was about thirty-five years old with a close-cropped haircut. It was difficult to tell whether he was of a blue collar or free spirit background. He interrupted me in a sarcastic tone: "Forget society's problems, Mullaney, and get back to your magnanimous offer to disclose the source and amount of all your contributors. Are you aware there is an ordinance now that requires disclosures of contributions?"

I was prepared for that question. "Yes," I said, "but it is totally ineffective because it doesn't require volunteer committees to divulge receipts and spending. Candidates get around the law by hiding behind volunteer committees."

The bobbing heads around the table told me I had scored a point. Unwisely, I did not accept victory. Continuing, I said, "Of related significance for you, the committee, is the embarrassment I may cause the city council endorsees next fall." They didn't understand. "If you endorse eight persons for the council next fall and me for mayor, it would be embarrassing to the council endorsees and ultimately to you, the endorsing body, if the leader of the ticket is the only one of the nine who discloses the source and amount of contributions."

They did not take it well. I wanted to offer it as a taunt to those not committed to the fight against influence-peddling, but it was interpreted as self-laudatory.

Next, my friend David Shapiro wanted my position on government funding—Catholic taxes—for parochial education. It was a reasonable question for a Jew to ask of a Catholic. I'm not sure how my answer was accepted. It had something to do with the equitable return on my tax dollar.

Mrs. Durwood, another of the First Amendment Democrats, posed a sensible question about the strengthening of zoning ordinances to protect homeowners from rapidly encroaching apartment complexes. I had expected her to phrase a pornography question in such a way as to force a reactionary answer.

One of the women on the right side of the table wanted my opinion of a musical playing in town. It may have been a loaded question from someone familiar with my complaint to the city attorney. I let her know I objected to the mockery of the Eucharist in the so-called play. Blank faces.

While waiting for someone else to speak, I told of my interest in getting a professional basketball tenant for the new city auditorium. That perked up a few of the males.

Then I made a statement on millage authority. No one except Ulric Anderson knew what I was saying. Attempting to draw him out, I asked, "Is that correct, Ulric?"

Playing the actor, he replied, "Who, me?"

A stout man, past middle age, wanted my position on welfare. I was unable to guess whether he was a hardhat-redneck, certain that all recipients cheated, or if he was sincerely interested in those in need of public assistance.

I did not equivocate: "Of the fifteen million

people on welfare in the United States, nine million are children, one million are blind, and most of the rest are over sixty-five or mothers of dependent children. Certainly, there are some fathers who won't work and some women who make fraudulent claims, but the general condition of our welfare programs is reasonably good."

The man was satisfied and I was pleased. I'd like to have orchestrated about welfare at the top, but fixed-income people have been so conditioned to castigating their own, I'd probably have been resisted by the lower middle income committee members.

Darcy Braun, wearing oversized glasses and braids, sat passively thus far during the screening.

An effeminate fellow said, "What do you think about the Massey Rifle?"

He was referring to the purchase by Burlington police of a new kind of weapon. While Vin Norris was mayor, several nincompoops had camped out in the mayor's office for a long weekend, protesting the rifle's purchase.

"I'm not exactly sure what you mean," I answered, "partly because I don't know enough about the rifle."

In this, I was being truthful. I had an idea the bullet was most discriminating, as contrasted with the spray of a shotgun shell. Maybe that wasn't the desired effect, but I didn't understand why bystanders should have to risk being hit.

"But this is what they use in war," he said persistently.

I gave him a so-what look and he said no more. I overdid the ignorant role. He failed to relate the rifle to the cause of the sit-in at the mayor's office and I did not volunteer a comment.

I knew that if I said I'd have kicked out the protestors in two seconds, and gave as my reason the mayor's need to conduct the business of his office, I'd have been branded an unfeeling, law and order fink.

By remaining quiet, I had committed a sin of omission. It was ironic. When I entered the screening room, I was concerned about saying something I didn't believe in. Certainly, being quiet was as serious a moral breach. A Pilate non-act.

It was apparent Carleton Majors was readying a long-planned cheap shot. He shifted uneasily in his chair as he inquired rhetorically: "Being a legislator and not an administrator, how much do you think your lack of experience will injure the City of Burlington before you sharpen up?"

"Since you mention the capacity to injure," I said, "how would you estimate the damage you're doing to the Democrats with your presence here tonight as a double agent for the Republican party?"

"That's the most scandalous statement I've ever heard," Carleton screamed. "I demand an immediate apology, Mullaney!"

I expected Smythe to halt our exchange, but he and the others on the committee turned and eyeballed Carleton.

I took the letter from my inside coat pocket and gave it to David Shapiro, the only person around the table whom I trusted.

"This letter bears the letterhead of the First National Bank of Burlington and the signature of the bank's board chairman. I'll now ask Mr. Shapiro to read the contents to the committee."

As David perused the spy request letter, Carleton stood abruptly and said to the chairman, "That won't be necessary. I'll be leaving now."

If other screeners had intentions of taking swings at me, my brief flurry with Carleton probably silenced them with shock. I had hoped to hear from the abortionists around the table so that I could call them progenitors of the Fourth Reich.

There wasn't one word spoken by this Democratic group which touched on labor or race, the two most prominent reasons I had become a Democrat.

I was sure I hadn't gained a single vote from this body.

For the last question, I was ready. It's asked of every candidate for any Democratic endorsement. "Will you seek this group's endorsement if you run for the vacant office of mayor? (I wasn't a formally declared candidate and probably wouldn't be since it was not an at-large election.) My very presence told the gathering whether I was seeking their endorsement, so it appeared as an innocent and unnecessary question. But if a candidate said yes and then did not get the endorsement, he just promised himself out of running for the office. Committee members liked to construe one's answer as a promise of support for the winner of the endorsement. At least, that's the way it has been in the past.

I decided to stick in the needle a little bit. "Well,

there is this problem of whether you can back me if I disclose the identity and amount of all contributions. Until you let me know, I can't give you an answer as to whether or not I'll seek your endorsement." They were confused and I was happy.

Chairman Smythe gaveled to a halt the buzzing conversations around the table. "Your time's up, Mr. Mullaney," he said. "Thank you for appearing before the screening committee. We will contact you."

The night air was invigorating. I chose the long way home along the River Boulevard, trying to recall the telling looks and cluing responses in the screening room. It was an experience such as I had tonight that made me long for Ann Marie's companionship. We would have gone to a coffeehouse and conducted a two-person poll on the state of my campaign.

VII

Not unexpectedly, and without fanfare, former Deputy Commissioner Clark Mathews was voted unanimously into the vacancy left by Commissioner Walter Manville.

That meant one secure mayoral vote for Manville, with seven publicly uncommitted votes remaining. A simple majority of five was needed to win the election.

Politicking had nearly stopped on the Democratic side. Jack Clay had been trying to find out if Griffin and I were the only serious labor candidates. His only success in divining information was in hearing from diverse sources that a fairly unknown feminist had a chance of getting the Democratic party endorsement for mayor.

Vin Norris met me in the city council chamber for the accelerated swearing-in ceremony of Clark Mathews. Many spectators shook hands with Mathews, who for the first time in his life was thrust into a position of power. It was my hope this debtor of Walter Manville, and now Constance Wetherby, would be unpersuasive and not a fulcrum in the political jury of which he was the newest member.

For privacy, Norris and I went across the street

to the coffee shop at the Chaix-Gordon Hotel. Even though Vada Griffin was a labor favorite, I experienced a feeling of anticipation when Vin began to unravel the mysterious goings-on at the Labor Temple.

"When I asked if labor had made its selection," Vin said, "I was made chairman of a coordinating committee of labor and Democratic party representatives who had been unsuccessful in deciding upon either laborite Vada Griffin or the party's Liz Deering as the joint choice of the committee. This was my first knowledge you were not the front runner for either group."

"We met early this morning and Boss Kane started out with Bismarck diplomacy. He cracked his fist on the table, declaring to the party that labor had a volunteer worker on every city block and already enough money for next fall's mayoral election."

"What was the stance of the party representatives," I asked. "Did they get tough in return?"

"No, the courteous response of Archibald Smythe, the party's screening chairman, was translated as capitulation. One of the other Democrats sensed this and suggested in a stronger way that an evaluation be made of each group's candidate."

"Boss Kane pointed a finger at the semi-circle of Democrats and told them, 'The only choice you have is how strongly you support our candidate.' I spoke to the Democrats privately and recommended they drop Liz Deering and advance your name, Connor. After all, Boss Kane is your friend. But no, they all thought you were too conservative."

"None was high on Deering, but the same went for Griffin. Everyone was bitter about Kane's sledgehammer approach, so, do you know what happened? Each of them stalked out."

"Does that mean Vada Griffin is the Labor-endorsed Democratic candidate?"

"Yes, I guess so. Before leaving, they authorized me to inform Kane they were dropping their support of Mrs. Deering. In this way, Griffin won the committee's crown through the back door."

The information from Vin Norris wasn't what I had hoped for, but I was determined to stay in the race until Mayor Baker's successor was chosen. With only three sometime laborites on the city council, I still was convinced Vada Griffin could not get a majority of the eight votes.

I left Vin and called Republican Commissioner Bert Peterson again. He listened to my request for his vote, but would not converse.

The other Republican on the council, George Zachman, was less friendly on the phone this time, saying, "There's really no sense in going to lunch, Mullaney, or getting together, or even calling me."

The Republicans were turning me down because I was loyal to the Democratic party, the organization that apparently didn't care if I existed.

With three acknowledged Independents on the council, two Republicans and three Democrats, I hoped Peterson and Zachman realized I could be hurt by seeking their votes.

The only reason I was courting the Republicans was because of my belief that too much contact work was better than too little. One could never know all the variables, the ulterior reasoning, the unexpected alliances.

Standing outside the Merchandise Mart was Jamey Peters, perennial state senate candidate. He was avoiding me. In one sense, I was happy as I wouldn't have to face his usual histrionics, but it bothered me that he didn't offer help when I needed it. He knew I was not of the radical left to which he belonged; but that didn't prevent him from begging my aid at plant gates when he ran for the senate. Nor was he shy about euchring one hundred dollars from me for his last campaign. Why didn't I expect his snub? If I had looked at politics as a self-serving endeavor, I'd have been a more efficient state representative.

— ★ ★ ★ —

Both of Carroll Dupre's automobiles were in the driveway of his old mansion, so I was sure he was at home.

Dupre was the prime mover in Constance Wetherby's first council campaign. I respected him because he was as blunt as Bart Countryman.

I drove past his house and called him when I arrived at the restaurant where I was meeting Jack Clay.

Predictably, Carroll was frank with me. "They're going to *announce* Walter Manville's election to the mayor's office in the next couple of days," he said. "It's going to be popped out casually at a city council meeting."

My fear of something underhanded taking place

was evidently well-founded.

Not knowing who were the parties to the deal, I didn't know how to combat it. It seemed senseless at this juncture to re-contact any city council members.

The newspaper was my only recourse. If its City Hall reporters had some hint of an illicit agreement, the *Courier* might attempt to expose it before Manville was seated. That thought calmed me. Maybe it was false security, or naivete, but I knew that a strong editorial could fill the council chamber with unruly voters, and it was possible nothing more would be needed.

I was aware my message would sound strange, but I phoned *Courier* editorialist Barry Siler. "He won't be in for an hour or more," his secretary informed me.

In an almost absent-minded way, I said, "I have a hot tip I thought Barry might want."

Seasoned for that type of caller, the secretary said immediately, "Then you want to speak with Harry Wolfe."

I was loathe to confide in the managing editor. He already may have known of the scheme and not wanted to disturb it.

Wolfe said hello and asked for my information, so I capsulized what I knew. "An insider reported to me that a new mayor has been selected, and I believe the price is the cable television franchise." He did not interrupt. "It's supposed to come up during one of the next few council meetings, and I don't like it. I'm sure my view is not perfectly objective since I also am a candidate for mayor (muffled laughter from Wolfe), but I thought you'd want this lead, nevertheless."

I didn't overstep my invisible boundary by telling the editor he should smite the miscreants in print.

Wolfe was friendly but noncommittal. He didn't admit to his paper having any knowledge of the deal, merely saying, "We'll look into it."

I felt foolish, for now I was certain he wouldn't do anything with my information. In a way, though, I was relieved. The *Courier* was my best and last appellate court, and if its writers did not act, it was their failing, not mine.

I called Barry Siler later to hear of Wolfe's reaction. The switchboard operator said Siler was in conference, but was taking his calls.

"No, Harry didn't mention anything," he said. That's what was done with my tip. Nothing.

I repeated to Siler what information I was given and the reliability of the source.

His only comment was, "What did you expect from a bunch like that?"

Was he acknowledging what was taking place while at the same time indicating his managing editor asked him not to editorialize? Now with the *Courier* obviously not interested, I was powerless to stop this outrageous betrayal of the public trust.

— ★ ★ ★ —

Two longtime Irish friends, Forrest McCabe and Derry Fitzmorris, thought I needed a respite from politicking, so they invited me to a neighborhood cocktail lounge. When we entered the anterior bar, I noticed Jason "Windy" Wetherby, husband of Commissioner Constance Wetherby. Even though he preferred the sobriquet, Constance was known to get vicious when her husband was called Windy. "Jace" was not acceptable to her, either.

I never was sure he knew my name, so I walked over and introduced myself. He was eating the olive from his martini. I ordered a blend and water as we exchanged pleasantries.

Windy was wearing an Hawaiian shirt hanging outside his bermuda shorts, even though winter had not conceded defeat yet. I wished I dared peer at his footwear to see if he was wearing sandals!

The wealthy owner of a third generation tugboat company was amicable and revealing. "My wife was a real bear, so I had to get out of the house."

I primed him with a vague-sounding question: "Have you heard about the council being influenced, so to speak?"

He didn't bite. "My wife was out of town. I haven't heard anything." Nor was he asking me to elaborate.

I imagined I was expected to believe his wife didn't make a long distance call to her deputy commissioner to find out what was happening on the home front. Because Constance and Windy were not poor, I doubted her entanglement with the TV combine. But more unlikely things had happened in Burlington politics. It even was possible that Al Kelder had made Constance the assistant instigator.

Windy Wetherby reflected on the many political battles he had been in. "Twenty-seven years ago,

Lindsay Ballard was our congressman," he said. "He really stuck me and I went at him in every way I knew. I made him a one-termer. He pulled something on me and I nailed him good."

Removing obstacles from his path by societally unacceptable means was not a great worry for Windy. He had been investigated by different law enforcement agencies at various times, but for unmysterious reasons, he never was charged with breaking any laws.

McCabe and Fitzmorris were in their own conversation at a table a few feet away from us. I continued to bore in on Wetherby and hoped I was doing it effectively. "Getting back to the vacancy in the mayor's office, Windy, is there any truth to your wife's knuckling under to the cable company?"

I had tapped the right vein.

"My wife remained quiet when she knew Marcella Baker was not going to finish out her term. She could see the bribe artists gradually getting to Marcella, knowing the Baker Enterprises were in severe financial trouble."

"How could Marcella's resignation help the television people?"

"By allowing their kingpin, Walter Manville, to take over the mayor's office and assume a stronger control of the franchise effort."

I wasn't at all satisfied. He was making an enormous charge against Marcella and it had to be challenged.

"As the head of a large corporation, Windy, you certainly don't accuse your employees of anything without proof. What proof and what facts do you have that Marcella took graft?"

"All I know is that the banks would have closed up her firms long ago if she didn't have silent collateral."

"That's a guess. Give me some facts."

I was trying to think of a reason Constance would want to injure the retiring mayor. I suppose she envied Marcella's holding the higher office, but that was not enough.

"Marcella Baker knew my wife was planning to run for mayor next fall, whether or not Marcella retired. By quitting before November and telling Walter Manville about it but no one else in city government, Marcella thus could damage Constance's chance in the at-large election next fall. Walter acted quickly by resigning before Marcella so that he would be eligible constitutionally to participate in the intramural election. He probably made it a condition of his involvement with Al Kelder's group that Marcella would be taken care of in the form of backing for her financially distressed companies. Thieves sometimes have loyalty, you know."

Wetherby took considerable pleasure in his derisive climax.

It was possible Marcella didn't have one of the autos supposedly supplied by Kelder because of her demand for bigger things, such as loan collateral. The first thing I wanted to determine was the source of credit for Marcella's companies. If it checked out, I would feel much better than I did now. Somehow, Windy's accusation had a ring of plausibility.

I lapsed into thinking about the stupidity of those who may have accepted autos and boats from Kelder rather than money. It wouldn't take a lot of investigation to track down the proof of the transfer of vehicle ownership.

All of this was ancillary to the purpose of my conversation, so I said, "Does your wife consider me a good candidate?"

He started backing off before I had completed my question. "When it was not popular to do so," he growled, "Vada Griffin supported my wife and took some abuse doing it."

"A minute ago," I interjected, "you told me Constance would not support any Democratic legislation and now you say she will support the party's candidate? Isn't she being inconsistent?"

"She'll give him her token vote as thanks. Don't count on it to go further."

"I'd still like to talk with her again. Will you tell her I'll call her?"

"No, you call her. She may think I'm trying to sway her. And she wouldn't go for that."

I had suspected Constance wore the family pants. Now I knew.

The subject was exhausted, so I got off the bar stool and drew my friends into our talk. Shortly, Windy disappeared through the rear door.

VIII

At nine-thirty in the morning I entered the City Hall office of Commissioner Constance Wetherby.

"No, I don't have an appointment," I answered a young man in a bargain store suit.

He went into a back office and then reappeared, stating apologetically that Mrs. Wetherby was not yet in the office. I was expecting her to have been at her desk early on her first day back in town.

Would I speak with the deputy commissioner, Lainy Ross? I said, "Yes," but for what reason, I didn't know. She couldn't help or damage my candidacy, and my oral largesse might reveal something it shouldn't.

Lainy Ross had a reputation of being an asset to Constance. Would I find her nice-looking, bright and efficient, as she had been described? Or would she be an insufferable goldbricker?

What I found was a charming brunette in her early forties with a face that broke into a natural smile.

Bart Countryman said I should expect a fashion-plate and I was not disappointed.

It was difficult to discern whether a cagey politician hid behind her smile. Though I addressed her as Lainy, she referred to me as Mr. Mullaney. Was that a high fence or her usual courtesy?

"I am so sorry, Mr. Mullaney. Mrs. Wetherby is not in. Is there anything I can do for you?"

She was fishing, so I brought up my favorite query: "Have you heard anything on some trades being made for cable TV votes?"

Mrs. Ross' expression did not change. "Yes, I've heard something about it. I don't know it it's true."

As long as she didn't equivocate, there wasn't much more to say without knowing which votes made up the majority.

"Do you know who will vote for Manville?" I asked. That was a bold, impertinent question. I was suggesting she tattle on her boss. She fielded it well by turning it back to me: "Do you have any ideas?"

I grinned as I shook my head from side to side.

Just then, Lainy heralded the arrival of the Wetherby family's pants-wearer. It was opportune for me. I had been ready to leave.

I pivoted to see the tanned face of Constance Wetherby. The deputy commissioner explained to Mrs. Wetherby that I was there to meet with her.

"I ran into Jason," I said. "Did he tell you?"

"No, I don't believe so."

As the commissioner sat down behind her desk, I thought she looked fifteen years younger. She must have had a facial and lost some weight, I decided.

Constance did not offer me a chair, but I slid into an upright visitor's chair on her left.

"I have a meeting at the fire department," she pressed. "How long will this take?"

"About thirty seconds," I said. That seemed to placate her, although her gaze said I'd better be snappy.

I offered a conciliatory opener: "I know your allegiance rests with Vada Griffin. However, I do want you to consider me as a compromise choice if there is a deadlock." No reaction. Okay, ma'am, I thought, you're going to get the big question. "I hear there is unanimity on Walter Manville for, ah, some outlandish considerations. Do you know anything about it?"

I had a feeling she was going to have me thrown out, but she stood merely, signaling the end of the conversation. I was tempted to kneel and kiss her hand.

When I got to the door of her office, I stopped and looked back at her, asking, "If there is no unanimity, is Talbot then the swing vote?" It was a little flippant and a little sincere. I really did want to know how Talbot was voting because, though I couldn't explain why, I felt his was the key vote.

The Fire Commissioner stared at me without answering, so I left her office with no more sass.

As I walked hurriedly down the marble corridor, I heard the urgency in Commissioner Wetherby's voice, "Connor! Connor Mullaney!"

She caught up to me, tugging at my sleeve.

"I'm not myself, Connor. Please understand. I

am having severe discipline problems with one of my sons."

Before I could reply, she circled and disappeared through a side door to her office.

— ★ ★ ★ —

I tried to stop Carroll Dupre as his stationwagon was pulling away from the curb in front of the First National Bank. He waved, oblivious of my interest to seek him out. Then, maybe he was glad I missed him. That way, he wouldn't have to release any secrets.

I called Dupre later at his home and asked if the sell-out was still on.

"Well, I suppose it is," he said, "but I haven't heard anything. I wish you'd call it something other than a sell-out, Connor. These things happen all the time in politics. I prefer to think of it as an understanding, an entente. Regardless of what we label it, however, nothing can be settled while Constance is in conference with the district fire chiefs. Her meeting could run into tomorrow or the next day."

That was the next thing to telling me Constance was the guiding force.

He wanted to get off the phone without getting into details and I didn't blame him. He was not only privy to strategy sessions, but may have taken part in the decision-making. I wasn't going to be put off so easily, though. I asked, "Is the majority of the Manville bloc made up of Independents and two of the Democrats or both of the Republicans? I'm assuming the three Independents are unified on Manville." Not letting him answer, I continued, "Is Sam Talbot the one Democrat who is hooked?" I posed that with the outside chance one Democrat, one Republican and three Independents comprised the majority.

I mentioned Talbot because he was pliable, gullible. Yet, he already was in trouble with labor and the Democrats. If his vote effected a majority, he could forget the powerful assistance of the labor-Democratic Party coalition in the future.

"Connor, you're assuming there are only five of eight votes for Manville," Carroll Dupre said. "We talked of unanimity and we may realize it."

Were all eight bought off? Did that mean the tough-guy approach of labor at the private meetings with the Democrats was an act? Of course, it was possible labor was sincere about its mayoral endorsee, but out of touch with the laborites on the council.

There was no sense in trying to pick Dupre's mind any longer, at least today. He was a pragmatist and I was of no foreseeable use to him. I believed he knew that neither he nor Constance could control me or romance my votes as mayor.

After hanging up, I meditated on the long-range motivations of Democratic commissioner Sonny Wallace. I doubted he could vote with Ellsworth Hayden and the other independents on the probable Manville bloc because he too wanted to be mayor; and joining hands on this matter wasn't a way to kick off a campaign. So why was Constance Wetherby, who also wanted to be mayor next fall, angling for Manville's success? The television franchise undoubtedly was part of the answer. So was the idea that Manville might be the most defeatable incumbent in November.

With Sonny Wallace, there had to be other considerations. During city council sessions, one of the strangest scenes was to watch Ellsworth Hayden exercise a psychological control over Wallace. Hayden intimidated the Democrat Wallace every few days and Wallace sat back in his seat and absorbed each barb silently. One of the reasons, I suppose, was that he thought he'd appear the winner in the long run if he didn't get into shouting matches with Hayden. The other reason simply was that Hayden was a quick-retort specialist while the younger commissioner found it necessary to prepare responses for nearly everything.

Would Wallace place in nomination the name of Vada Griffin? Manville? I thought it was more likely Commissioner Wetherby would nominate Griffin before she got on to her serious objective of electing Walter Manville. She owed Griffin a favor for his yesteryear support when she was unpopular. If she brought out Griffin's name, then Wallace could please the coordinating committee by seconding the nomination.

Commissioner Bert Peterson then could please the Republican party by offering the name of its eleventh hour selectee, anti-union man Gordon Mallory.

Ellsworth Hayden would repay his faithful head block worker, Jerry Cantrell, by submitting his name in token nomination. Cantrell also was a friend of Commissioner Talbot. Since there was absolutely no chance of Cantrell getting five votes, Hayden and Talbot could feel safe in their tandem support without risking Cantrell's election to the office. Then both could move on to their real candidates, having balanced the yoke of favors.

As I drove northward along London Road, I noticed Ellsworth Hayden's personal secretary sitting on a step at the entrance to an old warehouse which recently had been converted to an office building. Somewhere in town there was an old building that was renovated by cable TV applicant Al Kelder. I believed that I stumbled upon one of the pieces of the graft puzzle.

Further on down London Road I stopped on a hunch at the office of consulting engineer Darr Jones. He was as much the power behind Burlington Democratic candidates as was Bart Countryman. Though recognized as being closer to the party than to labor, Jones was trusted by the latter group.

Intelligent, confident and irascible, Darr Jones often was sought out by known and would-be candidates for his objective advice.

My decision to see him was made because he usually knew the inside word at City Hall.

I walked uninvited into his office.

"I know what you're going to ask," he said, "and I don't know any more than you. But the whole thing will probably help labor."

"No, no!" I exclaimed. "Labor didn't like Manville several years ago when its people screened him."

What I said was substantially correct, but did my emphatic tone infer a strong dislike by labor? I couldn't establish that.

"I'm aware he hasn't sought labor or party endorsement in recent years," Jones said, "but many of his votes and some of the legislation he sponsored have been helpful to labor."

So far, I was not convincing him the deal was ethically wrong or politically injurious. My next offering touched on Commissioner Wetherby's rationale.

"Constance does not want a woman or an endorsed Democrat replacing Mayor Baker, because if she runs in November, she would want labor and the party to be sympathetic to her independent candidacy. That would be the most effective method of corralling female Republicans, too."

My listener's logic chord was activated. "There would go the opportunity for liberal control of the council," he said.

Now that he was thinking more in my direction, I didn't want to let him go. "You don't believe Sonny Wallace would be a principal, do you?"

Jones really didn't answer. He uttered, "Hmm" a few times, as if mulling for the first time the prospect of Wallace's association with Al Kelder.

I couldn't seem to draw him out. Finally, he changed the subject.

"Say, how is Manville's health?"

"A friend of mine"—I was starting to get evasive myself—"said the growth on Walter Manville's lung was benign."

A smile broke across his face. "I question whether he ever had a serious problem. His condition might have been exaggerated to keep him from

80

being named to the difficult position of Commissioner of Administration. You know, it came up when Mayor Baker was making work assignments. Manville got the lighter job of Commissioner of Utilities and he was showered with public sympathy when the illness was mentioned in the *Courier*. I wonder if he ever was hospitalized."

Darr Jones had immediate recall of past events but didn't presently know if his buddy, Sonny Wallace, was bought by Al Kelder.

Just then, his secretary stuck her head in the doorway, giving him another assist in altering the subject.

"Did you tell Mr. Mullaney about Sonny Wallace's good forture?" she asked.

I turned to Jones and the red was inching upward from his neck to the top of his cheekbones. There was no way he could stop her without being obvious.

The secretary continued: "Sonny had this lake home next door to a big shot in the construction and cable TV business. Well, the guy was having his crew modernize his lake home and he thought as long as the workers were there they should fix up Sonny's place with insulation, new plumbing and light fixtures. He wouldn't let Sonny pay, saying he only wanted to be a good neighbor. He also added that it really didn't cost him anything personally since company materials were used."

Darr Jones peered at a letter opener as his secretary showed surprise when we didn't respond to her tale. She returned to her desk.

I closed the door. "Okay Darr," I said, "do you want to tell me about it?"

"You know as much as I. I told you that when you first walked in here."

I tried to leave his office as courteously as possible. There was the possibility he had been attempting quietly to thwart Al Kelder and his growing monster.

I couldn't find Commissioner Wallace yesterday or today. Last night at ten p.m. his attractive wife told me that he wasn't at home. Today, his secretary noted he was out of town for an emergency meeting.

Boss Kane was not in when I called. Neither was Vin Norris. I wanted to tell the receptionist at the Greeley Publishing Company that it was only one day before the big vote and the power brokers were not exactly waiting at my front door.

The Democratic party, labor, the Republicans and the labor-Democratic party coalition, none of these groups wanted me voted into the mayor's office. My contact at the Burlington *Courier*, Barry Siler, wouldn't even help me, and in fact was cool to me when I called.

I admitted it was time for a soul examination. One source of frustration was the thought that I had excellent experience at the capitol while none of my opponents, including ex-councilman Manville, seemed qualified for the job. I doubted any of them could intelligently scrutinize a revenue bond or plan a budget.

As importantly, could Manville, Griffin or Mallory provide leadership in creating innovative programs for city government? Or would they be caretakers, drawing a salary while advertising their integrity each campaign period? I knew the rest. Their word was their bond and their door always was open.

IX

Boss kane was expecting my morning call. Today, he leveled with me about some unnamed persons trying to forge a deal.

"They offered various things if we'd go for Walter Manville," he said.

I wanted to make certain I heard him correctly, as the rumor stopped and the fact started here. So I asked him to repeat his statement. He did and added his group was going to the bitter end with Vada Griffin.

"What does the bitter end mean?"

With a tinge of impatience, Boss said, "We're not going to compromise!"

I was not satisfied. "I don't know. Last night I heard that Sam Talbot is busting out."

"I don't think that will happen," the labor leader replied confidently.

I called Sonny Wallace's office again. "No, the commissioner is not in," a woman's voice said.

Hurrying, I searched the Chaix-Gordon coffee shop for politicians of any kind. No one was there.

I phoned Carroll Dupre. His secretary said he was in the council chamber. I hurried to City Hall and up the steps behind a bank of elevators. Dupre was coming out of Constance Wetherby's office. As I approached him, I noticed he was in pain. He had an old back injury which was exacerbated periodically.

"Is the announcement still going to be made?" I asked.

"As far as I know, yes. They're in there now." He pointed to the Wetherby office.

"Who are 'they'?"

"Wetherby, Hayden, Zachman, Talbot and Mathews."

He did not name Sonny Wallace.

It was ten minutes before ten. I looked into the chamber and spotted Sonny Wallace, the man whose name I thought Dupre would tick off with the others.

Wallace waved me over to his place at the council table. Before he could get into his phony welcoming routine, I said to him, "An unimpeachable informant told me the Manville trade still is on and that Sam Talbot is in the Wetherby office right now with the independents and Republicans."

Wallace gave me a quizzical glance. "Do you mean Sam is defecting?" he asked.

"Well, all I can do is quote from a person I believe to be telling the truth."

"Maybe I can nominate you, then."

I had waited patiently to hear those words, but before I could savor them, Wallace inquired, "How do you stand with labor and the party?"

Mr. Guile knew quite well how I stood with labor and the party.

I returned to the hallway and found Boss Kane. I let him know Commissioner Talbot was meeting at that moment with the antichrists.

He reacted casually, saying, "Oh, Sam will talk with anyone. I don't think he is going to switch."

There was no need to ask which pressure group would work on Sam if he did consider switching. And there was no doubt he was considering.

Boss Kane's thoughts were on labor's favorite son. "Walter Manville is being cussed at labor headquarters because he still is a candidate after he and Vada Griffin agreed to honor the choice of the business agents." That was my first indication Manville was screened by labor. He also must have met with the Republicans.

The head of the business agents continued: "Actually, it was Tubby Stewart and Lon Jepson pushing Manville's name and encouraging him to be interviewed by labor. In that way, they thought he could be finished off, because they knew Griffin had the business agents locked up."

As if anticipating my question, Kane said, "You are one of several compromise candidates in labor's eyes."

There was electricity in the air. The entire family of Walter Manville was in the chamber. Would they have come en masse today if they didn't already know who would win?"

Many state legislators and notables stood at the side walls rather than taking seats. Publicity-wise, they knew a television crew could spot them more easily if they were standing.

The council convened and balloting began quickly. Winona Smith, Constance Wetherby, Sonny Wallace and Sam Talbot voted for Vada Griffin. The first two commissioners must have held their breaths, not realizing they'd come so close to electing Griffin. Councilmen Peterson and Zachman cast their votes for Gordon Mallory. Independent Ellsworth Hayden chose his campaign manager, city auditorium head Jerry Cantrell.

On the next two ballots, Hayden changed his preference to Lon Jepson and then to his close friend, Ron Larey.

For the next eight ballots, Hayden voted with Republicans Peterson and Zachman when they advanced the name of Gordon Mallory.

In trying to embarrass Sam Talbot, Hayden voted for Talbot's cousin, bureaucrat Tony Talbot, on the twelfth through the thirty-ninth ballots. At an obvious impasse, Councilwoman Smith asked for and received a recess.

The more ballots taken, the better my chances were of being a compromise selection. However, that could be said of several candidates.

Democrat Wallace met with the two Republicans at independent Wetherby's office for forty minutes. Circulating the chamber was the rumor that the Burlington harbor authority vacancies were being used as bait.

I really didn't know what was going on. If the eventual winner had already been decided through the machinations of grafters, why would they be making offers to each other? I could understand it happening out in the open where the media and lay observers could be hoodwinked. But in private? I guess if it filtered out to me, though, it wasn't a secret, and that possibly was the key.

The city clerk announced that balloting would be suspended until six p.m.

Looking for elected officials, I crossed the street to the Covered Wagon, a popular place for politicians, professional athletes and married men desirous of meeting single office girls. I didn't enjoy the place. It was too provincial. Too Burlington. The same cliques occupying the same tables every day.

After not finding any politicians, I started out of the bar-restaurant when I saw television executive Jill Redman. She had been distant with me since the first time I ran for the state house. I then was on a panel show with the other candidate who had survived the primary election. Mrs. Redman was in charge of the show. One of her reporters had asked me a sarcastic question and I had replied, "Did you tell my campaign manager my news releases never again would be aired on your station?"

This live television disclosure had flustered the reporter, probably because it was as truthful as it was unexpected. In response, he had lied, saying he hadn't made such a statement. Jill smoothed everything over on the program, but I had no doubt she had written the format. Since that time, she has been courteous and occasionally friendly, but always aloof.

It didn't make any difference to me which way she reacted. I regarded her as an affable woman in a difficult role, a person whose friendship I never had an inclination to cultivate.

I had lost more respect for Jill when she accepted an appointment to Mayor Baker's municipal commission advisory board. The only conclusion I could make was that she was the willing dupe in the mayor's crass attempt to influence the media.

One of the men at Jill's table stopped me as I was walking out. He asked why I was getting mixed up with "those rotten commissioners."

"If you news people are aware of some larceny," I countered, "why don't you expose it? That is what you inferred, isn't it?"

Before he had a chance to answer me, Jill Redman spoke up. "We don't publicize rumors," she said sharply.

"Is that all that's holding you up?" I asked. "I can give you something to work on. Run over to Sonny Wallace's office and ask him why Al Kelder put fifteen thousand dollars of moderization into his lake home." All eyes were directed downward. "Go on, ask him. That is a fact, but don't take my word. Ask Wallace."

Silence prevailed, so I went on: "A journalist ignoring a solid lead can be more dishonest than a straight-out liar, Jill." I had hoped to address it to several tables of patrons and I thought I was successful.

Foregoing dinner, I arrived at the council chamber for the resumption of balloting. Commissioner Constance Wetherby submitted for the first time the name of resigned council member Walter Manville. She voted for him on the fortieth and forty-first ballots. Then she returned to Vada Griffin.

No new names were offered, and from the

forty-second through the fifty-fourth ballots, Griffin and Mallory each collected four votes. It was apparent neither side was going to give in, at least in the eyes of the public, so the second-most senior council member, Bert Peterson, called for another recess.

Former mayor Vin Norris stayed away from me in the many confabs springing up in the chamber after the session ended. I liked that because, contradictingly, I thought it meant he intended to stump for me. As he talked with the circular group of party chairwoman Geri Zanders, Commissioner Wallace and Democratic chairman Ulric Anderson, my name must have been mentioned, for all three of his listeners turned suddenly and looked at me. I didn't think it was a negative mention.

Vada Griffin, the man who held the Democratic-labor votes so securely through the fifty-four ballots, was standing alone. He was their pawn and didn't know it. The six-feet-six lumbering ox surely would have been more comfortable wrestling bears than seeking public office. His trousers sagged over his shoelaces; the narrow part of his tie was longer than the wide part; an uncontrollable spasm on the left side of his face showed the toll of his emotions.

With the voting halted, I went outside for fresh air. Buck Simmons, executive director of the Burlington Republican party, was leaning against a parking meter, inhaling deeply on a cigarette. With the events of the day, the time seemed later than seven o'clock.

When candidate Gordon Mallory walked towards Simmons, the end of his belt flapped lazily outside his suitcoat. As Commissioner Talbot ambled over to where the three of us stood, Mallory backed away and rejoined some men who were watching him. Talbot said hello to the Republican head, but not to me, his fellow partyman.

As Mallory left our earshot, I remarked to Simmons, "I'll bet he can get a healthy vote from the business community."

"Yes," Simmons replied, "if he'd stay away from the GRs."

The acronym stood for the Grass Roots party that sprung up in Burlington in the past three years. The members I've observed appeared to be excitable dunces. Mallory accepted the endorsements of both the GRs and the Republicans and each party was unhappy that he met with the other.

The GRs were blue-collar workers who were nearing the end of their home mortgage payments and were feeling quite establishmentarian. They were known for their belief in arbitrary budget cuts. Ironically, they had less distrust of Republicans than of the Democratic party and the Labor Temple, the latter organizations having been their catapaults to modest affluence.

— ★ ★ ★ —

It was seven-thirty when I telephoned the pompous, slippery man I could not trust. Was I compromising myself by even calling him?

Mrs. Ellsworth Hayden answered. "No, he's sleeping and it's his birthday. I hate to wake him. He's so played out. Can you call back in a half-hour?"

I called later and asked for the councilman. He was still sleeping. Call back in another half hour.

The next time I dialed, the line was busy, so I tried the children's phone. Mrs. Hayden answered again. I was embarrassed and apologized for being a pest. The pleasant lady didn't mind my calls, but said, "He'll get mean if I wake him." On his birthday, yet.

On my nine o'clock call, a gruff-voiced man answered. "H'lo," he said.

Though I knew it was the intimidator himself, I said, "Is Mr. Hayden there?"

Suspicious and noncommittal, he asked, "Who's this?"

Ignoring his question, I asked, "Is this Ellsworth?" He acknowledged that it was, so I said, "This is Connor Mullaney. Can we talk a minute?"

The commissioner was perfunctory. No, that wasn't strong enough. He was cold. "Listen, I'm on the other phone and there's no sense gabbing unless you can deliver the votes of Wallace, Talbot, Smith and one other, maybe Zachman.

"I think I can deliver Wallace's vote," I said proudly. "There's a possibility I can get Talbot, Smith and Zachman on my side."

There was no response. It was time to drop the name of his most knowledgeable braintruster. "I just talked with Perry Hale, Ellsworth. He suggested I call you." It worked. The veteran council member was immediately friendly. It was almost as if I were speaking to another person.

"Well, Connor,"—it was Connor now—"thinking is not enough. Do some checking and see if you can get assurances. If you can, get back to me."

Since Talbot and Wallace were doing whatever the Labor Temple was commanding, I phoned Boss Kane again. His chattels were reminded regularly that city elections were held every two years. If that wasn't reminder enough for politicians to remember their creditors, there were several delegations ready to assist their memories. Mrs. Kane said her widowed son would be away until after midnight. Many people had been calling, she said.

Next, I phoned Sonny Wallace. No answer. I dialed Marcella Baker's number and asked her a strategy question. I kept thinking I wouldn't mind if I lost the race because of the schemes of a crook, but if unskilled compaigning was the cause, I would not forgive myself soon.

When I called Wallace again, his wife answered. "He must have gone around the block for a walk. I don't see him in the yard."

It wasn't that I was blind to Wallace's avoiding me. I was merely determined to do everything possible to win and his rebuffs only strengthened my vigor.

— ★ ★ ★ —

Unsuccessful in finding Kane or Wallace the previous evening, I wasn't sure what situation I would encounter at the morning session in the council chamber. Because Kane apparently had been out of town, the coordinating group was either sticking with Vada Griffin or it had made an agreement to switch candidates before Kane left. I doubted the latter. If a compromise choice had been made, Kane would have led the delegation in trying to sell the new offering to the Republicans and independents on the city council.

I had learned that indentured city government appointees congregated at the east end of the chamber near the offices of the mayor and council members. Unencumbered appointees, mostly from past administrations, leaned against the railing at the west end of the room, which measured one hundred feet from east to west and sixty feet from north to south.

The seating arrangement for council members had the mayor at the top of the curve in the horseshoe. The microphone through which private citizens could address the body was at the open end. The speaker faced the mayor.

Not umbilicated to any faction, I usually stood against the railing at the west wall.

At a few minutes before the scheduled ten a.m. convening time, Boss Kane limped into the chamber with a pained expression on his face. He said he had been in a car accident while returning from his farm.

I wondered whether a communist could believe that a union leader only a few years graduated from the proletariat could own both a farm and a permanent home in the city.

The swelling of the injured leg showed through Kane's pantleg. He was a great kidder, so I didn't learn too much from him as to what had happened in the accident.

The labor chief pressed close to me and whispered that the coordinating group decided to stay with Griffin. My hopes were buoyed. I could relax for another day.

As Kane and I talked, Walter Manville entered through the double doors. He looked to his right, and seeing who was standing next to me, turned abruptly and headed toward the east wall.

Right behind Manville was Constance Wetherby. Her husband had been pacing the perimeter of the pew-like seats, obviously waiting for her. When he noticed her entering the room, he hurried, meeting her near the citizen's microphone. They huddled immediately, alternately whispering into each other's ear. Unseen by the couple, candidate Manville stood near them but far enough away so as not to eavesdrop. When Windy Wetherby backed off, Manville spoke to the commissioner. She did not say anything in return. Then Manville took a seat.

Constance normally was the first official in the chamber each morning and today was typical.

Commissioner Sam Talbot bounded into the room wearing fire-red slacks and an iridescent sportscoat. His attire must have had a calculated, conscious purpose. Sam's political flower had occasional difficulty blooming. Donning the loudest patterns was one of his election-year attention-getters.

Senior council member Ellsworth Hayden was not unaware of Talbot's lack of intellectual depth. Often, he tried to slip matters past Talbot when Mayor Baker was absent and he was presiding, only to be surprised by the junior commissioner's periodic mental agility, and temper. I had a feeling that, like his clothing, the purpose of his temper was to gain attention as well as to mask his most noticeable flaws.

The Commissioner of Police, Talbot was a successful businessman, with department stores and other interests. He lived in an expensive home in the elegant South Birch section of Burlington.

Standing with Walter Manville was a young, well-dressed man I had not seen previously. Had Manville been so certain of the victory that he promised an aide position to someone?

Almost as if on cue, Vada Griffin and entourage marched into the council room at exactly ten o'clock. All four men were muscular in appearance and ill at ease in business suits. Art Suter was one of them. He was the business agent for the scum skimmers at the sewage plant.

I knew only one of the other men with the candidate—Slick Jackson—who has had stiff annual opposition for his job, mainly because he believed reasonable offers from management should be accepted without a lot of nonsense.

Now, as chairman of the legislative search committee for the Labor Temple, Jackson commanded some real strength. Even though there were only three labor endorsees on the city council, independents and Republicans occasionally acceded to labor's demands, simply because Burlington was recognized as a working person's town. If Art Suter or Slick Jackson wanted to usher someone into a vacant public office, their clout and respect would go a long way toward assuring a good hearing for their prospective appointee. That would be in a normal situation. Here, in a setting nearly unprecedented in Burlington's political history, it was doubtful that the labor leaders could triumph. Citizens sympathetic to labor were not voting.

Furthermore, Jackson had abandoned his normal astuteness and was pressing too hard for the election of his friend, Vada Griffin. He seemed to have been too close to Griffin to grasp the reality of a hopeless uphill fight.

The council came to order a few minutes after Griffin's group arrived. Two ballots were taken. Four votes for Griffin, three votes for Mallory, one abstention. There was no change. Both sides were publicly entrenched in their positions.

Commissioner George Zachman asked for and was granted a recess until after lunch by acting mayor Hayden. No objection was made by other council persons.

Zachman and Hayden walked directly to the latter's office. Four reporters surrounded Commissioner Wetherby. Sonny Wallace was explaining something to a *Courier* reporter. He must have felt silly retaining a serious facade while not voting his own hand.

Mrs. Wetherby left the reporters and went over to the other side of the chamber to confer with Commissioner Peterson. The two rarely had anything civil to say to each other. It wasn't a matter of dislike. Constance just didn't care to be seen with a Republican and Bert didn't want to associate with an independent.

Bert Peterson had difficulty expressing himself. Essentially a kind person, he would scuttle needed sidewalk legislation rather than allow an elderly homeowner to be injured financially.

He was a victim recently of an untrue, below-belt assertion. Speaking to union leaders at a luncheon, a Democratic district judge labeled Republican Peterson as "unbelievably stupid." A constituent hearing the comment might have believed the judge if he heard how inarticulate Peterson was at some of the city council meetings. But he once had been a university professor, so I treated the remark as blindly partisan.

As Commissioner Wetherby came over to meet with Peterson, I didn't notice until later that the third person present was Republican executive Buck Simmons. Wetherby spoke demonstrably with Peterson, but I was standing far enough away so that I didn't capture the gist of the conversation.

A few minutes later Simmons started to leave the chamber. I quizzed him on what was said and he indicated it was only sparring. Though he knew I was a Democrat, we shared a mutual respect for each other. Bright and honest, Simmons bore resemblance to former mayor Vin Norris.

As Boss Kane was leaving, Ulric Anderson was entering. It appeared they passed without speaking. Anderson waited for Wallace, as did I. I kept my distance, though, so I could talk alone with the commissioner.

Anderson and Wallace buzz-buzzed for a long period, maybe fifteen minutes. Twice Wallace looked back in my direction near the reporters' cubicle. His looks were not accompanied by his customary wave and smile. When the council chamber was packed, his acknowledgement was valuable. Another Democrat or just plain constituent getting the big wave from across the crowded room caused visitors to turn and stare at the important personage whom Commissioner Wallace condescended to greet. It always worked. Wallace knew this, of course, and used it at every city council session.

The conference between Wallace and the Democratic chairman lasted so very long that we three were the only ones remaining. The way they muffled their utterances with no one to overhear them except me was tangible evidence I was being treated as the party leper.

As they left, one behind the other, Anderson put on his trained grin and said, "Hi, Connor" as if that were the first knowledge he had of my presence in the room. Wallace didn't bother to say hello.

A newswoman reentered the chamber as we moved toward the doors. Wallace said to the reporter, "I just got my orders to go to a meeting," pointing at Anderson. Truly, that was the case. He was as much a puppet as Talbot, but for different reasons. Talbot merely wanted to be reelected to the council. With Wallace, the *Courier* was backing him so strongly that he could possibly win reelection to the city council without the labor-party endorsement. But reelection to the council was no longer satisfying. Wallace reportedly wanted higher office. Eventually he hoped to be appointed United States Senator by Governor Jacobs if Senator Huntington Hantley won the presidency.

As we departed the council room, Wallace was

going to ignore my obvious attempt to talk confidentially with him, so I said plainly, "Sonny, can I speak privately with you?"

At that, Anderson stepped off in the direction of the elevators. Wallace stopped, but the message was written on his face: "Hurry, I have important things to do."

He listened to my fatuous entreaty in which I asked for his vote. But I thought, just as with the salesperson, if I didn't ask for the sale, I wouldn't get it.

I suspected, though, that he either didn't have a choice in the matter or that he considered my candidacy a threat to his future.

I asked Wallace if there were an opportunity for my name to be brought forward as a compromise candidate. He replied, "Yours is one of six names being mentioned." That's all he would say.

As he walked away, I was surprised to hear him tell a broadcast reporter that various trades were being discussed.

While Wallace was being interviewed by the reporter and Ulric Anderson was conversing with someone unknown to me, I peered about to see what types of people had been interested in the election proceedings. One young man was noticeable immediately and apparently he intended it that way. He wore a ten gallon hat in a building that was hundreds of miles from ranch country.

I had never seen him in Burlington political circles. Remembering that one of the cable television groups entertaining city council members this past week was headed by Oklahoman Lawrence Terrell, I decided that that fellow could have been attached to Terrell's retinue. He was with four other men. We all were in the same elevator. An older man was steering the group. After a silent ride, the men poured out onto the marble floor at street level. I listened for a southwestern accent, but I didn't hear enough words to make a determination.

Two of the five men were talking animatingly and simultaneously. I walked over to be near them. They stood in a circle a few feet from the south revolving doors of City Hall. Acting as if I were searching for someone, I backed up to them and tried to watch peripherally for any hint my purpose was detected. I was successful in noticing one of the men studying me, so I exaggerated my panoramic gaze. It worked. They spoke as if they had privacy.

"Each of us will contact a separate council person. Get to the point right away by telling them Gordon Mallory is still the best candidate. Don't be afraid to apply a little muscle. Politicians only listen to power, so let them know how much influence our organization has. Now, among yourselves, decide which will be your follow-up contacts."

The listeners were silent, so the older man elaborated. "Don't you remember? We agreed to an assignment of one council member for we five and the three who couldn't make it to the city council session. Then, we decided each of us would contact a second commissioner, preferably by personal visit."

There were disappointed looks. Belief in a candidate was one thing, but doing the leg work was another.

This certainly was a letdown! After all, I expected to tap the conversation of wealthy and conniving Oklahoma television executives and all I got was a small-minded group of Mallory supporters. I should have known by the grubbiness of their suits. Those men had to be from the Grass Roots party.

It had been announced that the city council meeting was recessed until two-thirty in the afternoon, ostensibly so the commissioners could meet in private to avoid the public ear.

I lunched alone to ruminate the morning's developments. Wallace was the only council person Constance Wetherby heeded. Hence, if Constance and Clark Mathews, her debtor, decided not to provide the fourth and fifth votes needed to push the labor candidate over the top, Wallace then might present her with a bipartisan hopeful, someone acceptable to both the labor-Democratic committee and to her and Clark.

With there being no question now that Wallace was avoiding me, my chance to succeed Marcella Baker as mayor of Burlington appeared to be moribund.

I doubted that Ellsworth Hayden was aware of Wallace's aim for higher than local office. Yet, that might be underestimating Hayden's shrewdness. A year ago, I would have laughed at anyone describing him thusly. But not now. He used words of which he didn't know the meaning; he examined many matters subjectively because of his great ego demands; he was more often undemocratic than solicitous of the council's and the public's wishes. Nonetheless, I guessed that his knowledge of and ability to implement the most important provisions of the city charter probably paralleled his sagacious capacity to know the intent of his opponents.

X

At two-fifteen I returned to the council chamber to witness the next act of the charade. A typewritten note was taped to the double doors. Its message was terse: "The two-thirty council meeting has been cancelled."

Momentarily, I was suspicious that an irresponsible person had affixed the note to the doors. That's what politics can do to a person.

The assistant city clerk came into the chamber shortly after I did. I asked if the note was true. He said it was, adding, "But I don't know what caused it to be cancelled."

As recording secretary, his interest most likely was in being accurate, not in hearing the rantings of city leaders.

I wanted to know his opinion of the state of the voting, but he was uncommunicative.

None of the elected officials was present in the chamber. After receiving assurance no meeting would take place, I did not leave. It was like being at a fire and staying on after the chief told bystanders everything was under control. Unscheduled excitement always was a possibility.

I wondered why Vada Griffin and one of his followers showed up. Obviously, he was not informed by labor-Democratic leaders that the council members would not convene at two-thirty. I only could conclude that he was an *intentional* impasse-candidate the coordinating committee exploited until it could arrive at a true bargaining point with the Republicans and independents; or else the majority of the coordinating group was in cahoots with the TV combine.

Griffin and his supporters wore positive-thinking buttons on their lapels. "We will win today" was their preachment.

Griffin had not seen the note on the doors. When informed the meeting would not be held, he said in a tone consistent with his button's message, "It's nothing to get excited about." Almost immediately the unswelling masses were pacified.

Vada Griffin's most polemic ideological rival, Republican Gordon Mallory, perhaps also an impasse candidate, entered the chamber through a semi-private door to council offices. He was not aware the meeting had been cancelled, of course, or he wouldn't have been present.

For all eight of the people in the council room to hear, the candidate said, "Don't they know this is important?"

I didn't think he really could be serious. Didn't he know the very reason the commissioners were not there was because the matter was extremely important? Couldn't he comprehend that the commissioners at that very moment were in some secret place trying to barter for the seat? Or trying to make a deal appear legitimate?

DECISION AT BURLINGTON

— ★ ★ ★ —

Jack Clay telephoned to tell me there would be another evening session. On my behalf, he wanted to contact the aircraft workers' head, Tubby Stewart, and Governor Jacobs for the second time around. I nixed the last because of our disagreement and my walkout at the governor's office. With the former a contact would not be harmful, although probably useless.

As a longtime friend of the governor, it would normally be reasonable to assume Clay could influence Jacobs. But I certainly had killed any chance of that when I was at the capitol.

I called Boss Kane at his home. He said the Labor Temple was releasing a statement to the media saying its members were staying with Vada Griffin. That was what I wanted to hear. Griffin never could get a fifth vote, so my chance of being a compromise selection therefore was enhanced.

Kane's knee was still bothering him from his accident two days ago, so I offered the name of an orthopedist.

The conversation turned to another nonpolitical subject before I asked if I were being considered presently as a substitute choice. Boss Kane skirted the question by saying, "We're going with Griffin today," with emphasis on today.

I leveled with him about Sonny Wallace being distant with me.

Kane was reflective. "He's going through a difficult period. Commissioner Wetherby is trying to swing Wallace to Manville. And the coordinating group is attempting to keep him committed to Vada Griffin."

Constance Wetherby would not be paying Wallace's campaign expenses next fall and in all the other elections—as labor would—so I expected Wallace to gravitate to Griffin.

Boss Kane said, "We should have realized the council selection was going to take some time."

He was referring to the arguments occurring at each coordinating committee meeting between people who were not aware the rest of the political world may have had other ideas as to the best candidate. I wanted to suggest to Kane that if the labor-party group had had a more qualified candidate initially, the suspense now might be over. I held my tongue. It was nearing seven-thirty, so I said I'd see him at the council meeting.

When I entered the chamber, Commissioner Wetherby was berating Ellsworth Hayden. She called the council's temporary presiding officer a dictator and herself an honest person. In case it didn't sound believable, she repeated the last portion: "I am an honest person." Everybody in the room was embarrassed except her.

A woman with a storybook background approached the podium. She said to the council persons, "Your new citizen advisory committee on crime has everyone on it but a former criminal."

The speaker appeared to be an eccentric. In her seventies, she wore a disarrayed blouse and skirt and talked with a lisp.

There were ten or twelve older people who sat

at council meetings every day. One had a shopping bag he carried everywhere, even if he moved only two feet. I assumed the woman at the podium was one of those regulars, vital one day, apparently senile today. Most of the eccentrics occasionally taking the microphone were told by Ellsworth Hayden either to sit down or leave. I was waiting for a rude remark from Hayden, but he acknowledged immediately the woman and her message, saying, "Sorry about that oversight, Martha. I'll take care of it right away and you can consider yourself on the committee."

The strong, defiant jaw was not as noticeable as in the past, but now I knew the elderly woman. She was Martha Larrabee, shoplifter nonpareil. In recent years the reformed criminal aided police in solving difficult cases while employed locally by a department store security detail.

The response was typical of Hayden's quickness. He appraised the soundness of Martha's idea; he recalled the number of persons already appointed to the twenty member committee; and he must have contemplated the makeup of those presently on the committee to determine whether they could work well with the ex-thief.

Walter Manville came over and stood next to me along the west wall. "Are you still interested in this business?" he asked. I didn't answer him. After the morning newspaper article in which Ellsworth Hayden was quoted as saying he tried to get the candidacy of Manville disallowed on grounds of ineligibility, Manville probably was intent on knowing whether I had stepped a notch closer to being selected. I did not mention the article, knowing he would.

The former commissioner commenced by calling Ellsworth a bag man. "You know, I had a violent argument with him in his office. He thought he'd tell the media his version but he didn't realize I made out a release of my own."

Just then, a *Courier* reporter joined us, but directed his attention to Manville. "Anything new since this morning?" he asked.

"I've talked with Commissioner Zachman," Manville said, "and I'll get it today or tomorrow at the latest."

Our elbows still touched as we leaned against the railing at the west wall where the unindentured stood.

The reporter halted Manville's bravado. "Have you talked with the president pro tem since he tried to derail your candidacy?"

Manville flinched a weak "No" reply but came back strongly in saying, "but I'll get it tonight or tomorrow. I'm positive of that."

Boss Kane was within earshot, so I slid down the railing and asked him what the greater meaning was in seven commissioners quickly opposing Ellsworth Hayden when he tried to get Manville declared ineligible. "Does it mean Manville will be the labor-Democratic candidate to succeed their earlier choice of Griffin?"

Boss answered with a gesture before he spoke. "No, Ellsworth's strategy was to get Manville kicked off the ballot so as to pressure the council into breaking the deadlock and making an early selection."

"Who could argue with early selection?"

"The coordinating committee, that's who."

Boss said the coordinating group instructed council Democrats and laborites to approve a consulting fee for departing mayor Baker. Then the labor-party council members could take until the millenium to choose a new mayor.

Kane said the coordinating committee met again and decided to continue backing Vada Griffin, forgetting that he told me as much two hours ago on the telephone.

Tempers were showing, Kane indicated, and members were fighting among themselves. The group feared that if it offered a compromise choice, the dike would break and three or four candidates would flow through in a hurry with no success.

Kane evaded the question of whether Manville would be the group's first compromise selection, stating merely that a decision was made to stick with Griffin.

As we talked, the clerk was announcing a public hearing for cable television legislation.

When the reporter finished interviewing Manville, he joined Kane and I, saying, "No mayoral ballot is planned tonight. Commissioner Talbot is supposed to lead off with a motion to pay Marcella Baker a consulting fee."

Boss winked at me. His stooges were following orders and he loved it.

Commissioner Wetherby had a little surprise

motion first, though. She proposed that Commissioners Zachman and Wallace be appointed to the state transit commission, representing the City of Burlington.

The mayor pro tem interrupted, claiming there was no urgency to the appointments.

Wetherby and Hayden exchanged arguments as Wetherby's temperature rose. She said she wanted the seats on the transit commission removed from wheeling and dealing. But the very reason she brought forth the motion indicated an agreement had been reached with the prospective appointees backing down on some positions they had taken or persons they had supported.

The motion was seconded. With no discussion, voting began. Wallace, "Aye." Wetherby, "Aye." After a pause, Peterson, losing his seat, abstained. It was counted as a nay. Talbot, "Aye." Zachman, "Aye." Smith, "Aye." Already a simple majority. Mathews, "Aye." The pro tem did not vote and the secretary recorded it as the second nay.

What did George Zachman give away for the most important committee appointment the council could make?

Walter Manville approached Commissioner Talbot's chair. They whispered for a moment. Was Manville the reason Zachman's armor was penetrated? Was it the anticipated election of Zachman to the transit commission that caused Manville to be cocksure with the reporter? I doubted it. I had a pervading feeling that the council members were holding out for bigger stakes, such as a percentage of the net profits from cable television revenues.

I went over to where the salaried director of the state Republican party was standing. "It looks as if something underhanded has taken place," I said to Buck Simmons. "But do you think it could merely be a window to deeper and more extensive goings-on?"

Simmons agreed with his eyes looking away from me.

"Do you know anything about it, Buck?"

He was sitting in the rearmost row of seats. With a knowing but pleading stare, he said, "No, but it appears some opponents have stopped disagreeing."

There was no question who the principals were. The sellers were the Democrats (not necessarily labor) and the sole buyer must have been Zachman. More accurately, I should have said the sellers were Constance Wetherby and the Democrats. But that was just for the little transaction of the transit commission job which paid five thousand avocational dollars a year and statewide publicity, the type Sonny Wallace believed would be important to his future. To whom was the big sale made? Did the cable TV combine buy out Manville and Wetherby, with the bigger share going to Wetherby for getting Mathews elected to the council and Zachman appointed to the prestigious state transit commission? In short, was Wetherby being paid to implement the payoffs and Manville being paid to be the mayoral watchdog?

I wondered if Zachman promised only to vote for Manville and not for Griffin when he was appointed. I thought back to when Boss Kane said the following day was going to be the longest of Zachman's life. Kane had said labor and the party were going to phone and visit Zachman from one end of the day to the other. The promise of an appointment was to have been the bait.

There was no doubt it would cost Zachman. Quid pro quo. I couldn't imagine Zachman the conservative voting for Vada Griffin, a man steeped in union activities. But it had to be Griffin. When Kane said Zachman would be swamped by labor-party representatives, it would be made clear, certainly, that the objective was to put Vada Griffin in the mayor's office.

Commissioner Wetherby made another motion, this one to elevate Sonny Wallace to president pro tem of the city council, thereby attempting to circumvent that portion of the city charter which stated the senior council person would be the temporary mayor until a successor was chosen by intramural vote. It was just flak. Even non-lawyers in the room knew that. The parliamentarian quietly informed Constance her motion was out of order.

The *Courier* reporter had said Commissioner Hayden would emerge from his office as the motion was presented. On schedule, he walked out behind the east-wall seats and lowered his angular frame into the mayor's chair.

An aide spoke into Hayden's ear, presumably telling him the parliamentarian acted at the time he entered the chamber.

The plot called for Sam Talbot to offer a resolution for Marcella Baker to be paid a consultant's fee until a successor took over. Then, according to the reporter, Ellsworth Hayden would scream and shout about Talbot having some personal benefit from the resolution and that he should inform the electorate what it is.

The production went off as predicted.

In the council meetings I attended in the past few days, I was impressed with Ellsworth Hayden's logical and well-ordered arguments. Conversely, I was surprised and disappointed by the politically charged illogic uttered by his foremost antagonist, Commissioner Wetherby. As the elderly, the ill-informed and the drifters paraded daily before the microphone provided for private citizens, she played out a role as Commissioner Contrary by taking up with every faction, regardless of whether the respective complaints were sensible or ridiculous.

In accusing Hayden of intimidating those who dared to take the microphone, Constance was accurate. The temporary mayor usually was abrupt with the average lay person. The alert, senior commissioner always seemed to have the right answers, however. He was reputed to know the city charter changes better than anyone in Burlington. As an example of his ability, yesterday he cut down April Carter, probably the next most knowledgeable person in the city on matters relating to the charter. It was not even a contest between Hayden and the woman who labored three years in a volunteer capacity rewriting the antiquated charter. April was intelligent and organized, but Hayden shot logical holes in her arguments.

Constance continued the harangue. When she called Ellsworth a dictator again, the pro tem rose from his chair and stalked off to his office-sanctuary without a word.

Windy Wetherby paced endlessly from the outer offices to the council room. Then into the news room to bother reporters.

I could see that the night session was going to pass without any ballots being taken, so I hurried out of the chamber to a public telephone.

I dialed the number and asked the answering boy's voice for Mr. Dupre. With his ailing back, I counted on Commissioner Wetherby's alter ego to be at his home. When Carroll picked up the phone, I bluntly asked, "What did Zachman trade to the independents and the labor-party group?"

Dupre, recognizing my voice, said, "I don't know what you're talking about, Mullaney!"

Puzzled, I asked, "Didn't you hear? Zachman and Wallace were voted onto the Transit Commission tonight. It is very important as appointments go, but I feel that more must be involved."

Carroll Dupre was incredulous. "I left the council meeting before any appointments were even mentioned. They didn't pass that tonight, did they?"

"What difference does the timing make, Carroll? It sounds as if you knew it was going to happen, so let me inquire, what did Zachman give up? I'm looking for specifics."

"Zachman took it away from Bert Peterson, huh? I hadn't thought about that aspect, that there could have been upstaging within the Republican camp."

"Are you intimating there was no more than a selfish vote by Zachman to fill his own basket? And without any implications with the independents and the labor-party coalition? Or the television combine?"

Dupre expressed confusion as to Zachman's intentions. "He couldn't vote for Vada Griffin after what he said, calling Griffin an incompetent. How could he give Vada his vote after that?"

"Of course he couldn't vote for Griffin. Are you letting on you don't know Manville is waiting in the shadows?"

"Maybe, maybe. I won't know if that agreement has been made until tomorrow morning. I'll go to City Hall and find out as much as I can. I cling to the opinion that a long battle is ahead. And I'm left with the impression Zachman's teaming up with the independents and labor on the transit appointments was a separate, disjointed act on George's part."

"I can't buy that argument, Carroll. The labor-Democrat group and Constance didn't include Commissioner Zachman for brotherly love. They had to be given something in return. Incidentally, Sonny Wallace's placement on the state commission, as well as that of Zachman's, just isn't all the way to the bottom of the Wetherby bag of tricks."

I passed up a sandwich and a drink on my way home. As I drove along Tenth Street in the dark, I realized how tired I was.

XI

I MADE MY usual morning phone call to Boss Kane. His secretary said, "He's on another call. Can you wait?"

Soon, Kane came on the line.

"Is the mayoral vote going to be finalized this morning," I asked, "because of the transit commission appointments?" I didn't think I should allude to the cable TV cloud, mainly because I'd only be giving Kane something to deny.

"I don't know personally, Connor, but I hear *something* is going to be brought in this morning. I'm told it's Walter Manville, but that's secondhand."

"If you aren't getting this information directly, Boss, who is? The party? Oh, incidentally, who did Zachman make a deal with?"

"I didn't get it from the Democrats. I talked a few minutes ago with Ulric Anderson. He doesn't know whether it is Manville."

I pressed harder. "If you aren't getting the information first hand, from whom are you hearing about Manville?"

He was evasive. "From different sources. It was all over the downtown restaurants last night. It kept filtering back this way."

I was fairly certain Kane was withholding some

facts. "Boss, if Zachman didn't make a covenant with you and labor or with Anderson and the Democratic party, who was it with? The labor sympathizers on the council? I can't believe that would happen, can you?" My tone was slightly mocking.

"You know," Boss said slowly, "Constance Wetherby hates Ellsworth only a little more than she hates us. Now that the bus appointments have been settled. . ."

"You people didn't abandon Griffin, did you?"

He answered "No" immediately, so I couldn't believe Winona Smith and the two labor puppets, Wallace and Talbot, then could drop Griffin and side with Wetherby. What could she do for them? For Wallace, she could not provide the dream of holding national office as could labor and the party. With Talbot, she could not nominate him at a Burlington Democratic convention as could Boss Kane. There was an unknown factor with Winona Smith. She stayed some distance from labor and the party, even though she was endorsed by both organizations. Her rationale was that she needed the housewives and career women as badly as she needed the unions and the various Democratic clubs in the city. Winona believed many Republican women would vote for her if she were not too identifiable with the blue collar voter. Constance used much the same strategy. Still, I couldn't visualize Winona Smith, Sonny Wallace and Sam Talbot jumping ship to swing with Wetherby and Zachman to effect five votes for Walter Manville.

Bert Peterson couldn't have been involved. He

would not vote the same way as Constance after she bounced him from the state appointment. It certainly was not Ellsworth Hayden who was the cause of the rumors circulating through downtown. Hayden and Wetherby never would vote for the same candidate in this election. Never.

After my talk with Boss Kane, I called Carroll Dupre again. He had said last night that he was going to find out at City Hall what would happen, really happen, when the deal was finally sealed.

At nine-forty his secretary said he was still across the street in City Hall. I was at Bart Countryman's office and I instructed her to have Carroll call me back. I waited until ten-fifteen and the call did not come, so I concluded Constance was giving Carroll a thorough explanation of what was about to transpire.

The election of the mayor loomed as a big victory for Commissioner Wetherby. Or Al Kelder. Or the other cable TV stockholders.

One person didn't figure to be entangled in Kelder's web. That was Winona Smith. As honest as a nun, Winona may have been fed some lies for reasons to back Manville.

I arrived late for the start of the city council session. It was ten twenty-five. Commissioner Hayden usually conducted the boring business first and kept all spectators waiting for the daily lancing that was engendered by the election.

I was certain this morning I'd be safe in my tardiness, as the rumor about Manville's impending election success would have to be brought to reality by none other than Constance Wetherby. That is, if it were true. And if Commissioner Wetherby did bring the matter forward, her enemy, Hayden, definitely would delay its presentation until after the airing and disposition of all other items on the agenda. Anything to perpetuate the vendetta.

Hayden's dilatory intent was evident when he tried to have Walter Manville removed from the ballot with an allegation that Manville's resignation was improperly motivated. It was a juvenile accusation. No statute or ordinance said a council member couldn't resign for any reason he chose. The crafty Hayden knew that. He was trying to queer the proceedings for bargaining purposes.

There was an atmosphere of excitement when I stepped off the elevator. The crowd in the council chamber overflowed into the corridor. I made my way to the west wall with the help of a policeman who recognized me. There, I saw Carroll Dupre, so I hurried toward him, asking, "What has happened? Nothing on the election, I hope."

Sheepishly, Dupre said, "The pro tem just nominated Manville."

"You're kidding!" I exclaimed. "How could he? That's Constance's man, and they're not supposed to agree on anything. Furthermore, Manville is the candidate that Hayden tried to have removed from considerations. Was their so-called bitter argument contrived?"

Carroll listened patiently and replied, his answer not touching on the point I made: "Well, that's what occurred."

"You were going to tell me what kind of agreement was made."

"Ellsworth didn't pull anything," Carroll said. "He's tired of this whole thing. Council business was not being handled and he wanted to get back to normalcy."

I studied Dupre's face, wondering if he thought I would accept his explanation.

"You don't expect me to believe that garbage, Carroll." I wasn't angry, but I was disappointed he didn't think more of me than to offer a more plausible elucidation.

The temporary mayor was engaged in a lightly argumentative discussion regarding procedure. Finally, he said, "The council will take a five minute recess in my office."

All eight of the commissioners paraded out through the northeast corner door of the council room. With their quorum intact, they entered Hayden's office for a secret meeting, thereby violating a section of the city charter which prohibited closed meetings except in personnel hearings when a fired employee requested privacy.

Each time I was in the chamber, I searched for the wide-jowled face of Al Kelder, the cable TV king, but he was never in attendance. Controlling his marionettes while being away from their arena must have been difficult and unnerving.

The reason for the recess was hazy. But with Hayden's nomination of Manville, it seemed Hayden now was steering the Manville election effort.

If it were true that Hayden and Manville despised each other, why were they coming together and what instrument was causing it?

The recess was over in eleven minutes. All council members walked back to their seats as Hayden spoke into the microphone, "The clerk will call the roll."

The city clerk remained silent as he always did. His recording secretary read the roll, opening the dramatic and apparent finish to the speculation of who was to become Mayor Baker's successor.

Commissioner Wetherby's name was called first, indicating a clockwise recitation again would be used, even though the charter called for an alphabetical roll call.

Would Commissioner Wetherby vote for Manville now that Hayden had nominated him? Leaning forward to speak into her mike, she said, "Manville."

Sonny Wallace was next. He was ready and uttered "Vada Griffin." Maybe Sonny was not bought.

I considered the possibility I was witnessing a standoff, but then I laughed at myself. The council members did not go into Ellsworth's office to talk about disagreeing.

Bert Peterson was next. Would the Commissioner of Administration echo the mayor pro tem? Peterson was betrayed yesterday when his fellow Republican voted himself into Peterson's seat on the transit commission.

There had been conjecture as to whether the Republicans would stick together today. If Peterson voted the same way as Hayden and Zachman, I could conclude he was quietly enmeshed in the backroom intrigue. I was assuming the latter two would vote as Constance voted...and Walter Manville supposedly was her true candidate during the time she dallied with Vada Griffin. Previously, Bert Peterson had gone down the line with Gordon Mallory.

The secretary called Peterson's name. Softly, he said, "Mallory."

It was possible the election was not over. But then, I spotted Walter Manville's family, and they all were wearing celebration duds.

Sam Talbot's name was called. He would be thinking of Boss Kane's promise to nominate him at the city convention. Although Boss was known primarily as a laborite, his personal nomination at a Democratic convention was a virtual endorsement for a candidate.

Directing his gaze at Ellsworth Hayden, Talbot voted, "Griffin."

Two votes for Griffin. One for Mallory. One for Manville. Four more to be polled. Five needed to win.

Winona Smith left the council table and looked around the room for someone. She saw Boss Kane standing near me. Hurrying over to him, she seemed to give him a warning or threat. Kane was tense, but did not interrupt her. Every eye in the chamber was on Smith.

As she flung her arms out horizontally, with the palms of her hands turned upward, Kane thrust his finger at her nose, and nearly yelling, cried, "We're through with you!"

That was where coming from a tough neighborhood came in handy for Winona. When people reacted meanly, she almost enjoyed it. Not slowing or missing a stride, she returned to her chair.

The recording secretary called her name aloud and the Commissioner of Public Works, turning and staring at Boss Kane, said, "Walter Manville."

Two votes for Manville, two for Griffin, one for Mallory.

After hearing his name, Clark Mathews winked at Constance, his benefactress, and also said the name of Walter Manville.

It was difficult to imagine Ellsworth Hayden casting his vote for Griffin, the union man. Still, I could not fathom Hayden voting for Manville.

The president pro tem's name was announced through the scretary's microphone.

Harried and unsmiling, Commissioner Hayden said, "Walter Manville. Let's get this thing going."

Four votes for Manville.

Winona breathed something to Sonny Wallace that she seemed to think was immensely funny. Wallace did not laugh.

I was starting to believe Wallace was showing a long face for the benefit of the labor-party people in the audience. His true thoughts likely centered on Manville not being future competition for state or national offices. In particular, Wallace did not want a competitor for the labor constituency in the congressional district possibly being vacated by Cortland Peabody.

DECISION AT BURLINGTON

George Zachman was aware he was being watched by the overflow crowd.

As the secretary was about to call Zachman's name, Commissioner Peterson put his hand up in a stopping motion and leaned across his armrest to Zachman's left shoulder. They spoke movingly in loud whispers. I was too far away to understand them, at first.

Then the discussion became more heated and Peterson shouted to Zachman, "You're a traitor to the Republican party and to decency itself. You sold out!"

Commissioner Zachman took exception to the rebuke and as he began to explain his vote, whatever it was—and all assumed it would make Manville the mayor—Bert Peterson charged out of his chair and onto Zachman's swivel chair, with both men falling to the floor as the latter's single shafted seat tipped over. Some men standing nearby could easily have parted the wrestling Republicans if they hadn't been so surprised that the incident happened.

Peterson and Zachman rolled around on the hardwood floor with each man trying to throw punches. Spectators shrieked. Both men then got on their feet as Peterson let fly a jerky right hand punch to the left jaw of Zachman. Peterson needn't have recoiled, as Zachman fell backward, his head hitting a platform. There was a thud and blood spilled out of the back of Zachman's skull. He was unconscious and moaning.

A sheriff's deputy immediately pulled Peterson over into a council office and locked the door. A nurse was summoned swiftly from the city-county clinic to check Zachman's vital signs and resuscitate him if necessary. An ambulance was called. I cringed at the way his head had come in contact with the edge of the platform. Newsmen ran for their phones.

Commissioner Zachman had not uttered Manville's name, so there would be no new mayor today.

As soon as the stretcher was taken from the council room and the doors were closed, and with Peterson still out of sight, Ellsworth Hayden sounded his gavel and demanded order. He said he was extremely distressed for what happened, but claimed the balloting would have to continue. There was a gasp from the audience. Hayden said that the city charter called for a deputy commissioner to vote for the commissioner in case of the latter's incapacitation. He instructed the city clerk to call the Deputy Commissioner of Parks, Recreation and Stadia, Peter Holloway. The parliamentarian was quiet. A citizen spoke into the microphone, arguing that the balloting could not continue with Peterson gone and Zachman injured.

Hayden countered: "Commissioner Peterson has already cast his vote, so he is not needed as long as we have a quorum."

Deputy Holloway was very nervous, brushing dandruff from the shoulder of his dark suitcoat as he fitted into his boss's seat.

"The clerk will proceed with the roll call," Commissioner Hayden said.

The city clerk again was silent and his recording secretary read the name of Peter Holloway.

"I refuse to cast the vote to which only my superior is entitled."

The boyish deputy might have been technically correct, as no one had sworn him in as the acting commissioner. I doubted that the charter called for an automatic graduation of position.

Hayden now was nervous himself, uncharacteristically so. The stakes must have been big. He glanced furtively at his new friend, Constance Wetherby. She gave him a "Go ahead" indication in return.

"You have a duty to perform, young man, and that duty is to take over in the stead of the injured commissioner. Now, the city has work to do and you are holding it up. A mayor is needed, and right away."

"I still refuse to cast what could be the deciding vote."

More kindly now, Hayden queried Holloway, "Is it because you do not know how Commissioner Zachman was going to vote?"

"I know for whom he was going to vote. I'm not going to be a party. . .uh, I'm not going to take the responsibility, if you know what I mean, and you should," Holloway sputtered.

Hayden was in a quandary. He huddled with the parliamentarian and the city attorney. Then he took the mayor's mike and said, "I've just been informed by the city attorney that you will be derelict in your duty if you do not vote."

What nonsense! That meant anytime a council person abstained, it would be dereliction of duty.

Peter Holloway talked briefly with Commissioner Talbot. Then he took his seat, and holding the microphone with both hands, said, "I have decided to vote for Ma Hayden."

A burst of laughter erupted in the chamber. Ruth "Ma" Hayden, an eccentric council-room regular who claimed some kinship with Commissioner Ellsworth Hayden, rose and raised both arms in a victory salute. Nearly everyone in the audience cheered. One of her knee-length argyle stockings drooped around her ankle. Her uncombed, silvery hair moved lazily across her face.

The gavel of the temporary council president cracked. Ellsworth Hayden was very angry. He started to speak to Holloway when Commissioner Wetherby beat him to it: "This is not a comedy hall, Mister Holloway! We are here to perform the highly important task of finding a successor to Marcella Baker, someone who can know the ins and outs of a budget, one who can plan, intercede, pacify and mediate. So don't come in here with jokes."

Before the fire commissioner finished her remonstration, Deputy Holloway was gripping his microphone.

"As long as we're mentioning essentials, Commissioner, allow me to suggest to each candidate that he or she sign a declaration of non-involvement with any organization actively or prospectively doing business with the City of Burlington, and this would include cable television. My candidate, Ma Hayden, can do this. I know of another candidate who can state honestly that he is in this election for the purpose of bettering our city and not to pad his own wallet. You know who he is."

Holloway then pointed at me. It was an unanticipated, beautiful compliment. Although I had read some of Holloway's suggestions for city and state cooperative legislation, I really didn't know him very well.

"Spit it out, kid," Winona Smith said. "On my street, anybody who talks cute gets thrashed. Are you accusing me of wrongdoing because I voted for Walter Manville? Out with it, young man."

Peter Holloway steeled himself as he answered her bluntness. "I'm only saying that I concur when Commissioner Wetherby brings up the stringencies which should be considered while evaluating aspirants for the office of mayor. But let's not be hypocrites. How about including conflicts of interest when you consider disqualifying aspects?"

Ellsworth Hayden asked what seemed to be reasonable questions. "What makes this election different from any other? Where were you at the last one? Did you demand that waivers be signed then? During the middle of this contest is not the proper time to propose new legislation."

Holloway remained firm, telling the council he was sticking with his vote. While Republicans Peterson and Zachman were somewhat forgotten, no one knew what to do. Another ballot today obviously wouldn't go far.

Boss Kane opportunely motioned to Peter that he wanted to discuss the matter. If Holloway would vote for the laborite, Vada Griffin, and Kane could bring Winona Smith back into the fold and then convince the sequestered Bert Peterson that it would be merciful to drop Gordon Mallory and come over to the Griffin camp, Kane then could take the Wallace and Talbot votes and tally enough to win.

I had to believe Pete Holloway was in such a principled mood, though, that he wasn't going to change with any amount of convincing language.

Kane delivered his pitch and Holloway merely nodded, not in agreement, but as if to say, "Okay, I've heard your story. Now I'm going back to my seat at the council table."

Commissioners Wetherby and Hayden conferred with the city attorney for a lengthy period before Hayden bent over to his microphone and stated wearily, "No ballots will be taken for a minimum of one week. Nor will the city council meet during that period to conduct normal business on the agenda. I believe I am free to announce that the city attorney already has spoken with former mayor Marcella Baker and she has agreed to be hired on a part-time basis as a mayoral consultant, answerable daily to the city council. With the unfortunate incident that occurred today in this forum, it is best that little be said presently except that a quick recovery is wished Commissioner Zachman. I now will entertain a motion for a one-week adjournment."

Commissioner Clark Mathews immediately said "So moved" and Sam Talbot, who had been virtually quiet for several days, growled a second to the motion. The remaining council persons voted "Aye" promptly, joining Hayden, Mathews and Talbot in a desire to escape to a private corner where the wildest moment in city council history could be discussed openly.

Before I left the council chamber, I thanked Peter Holloway, not only for the compliment he gave me, but for halting at least temporarily the progression of Al Kelder's cable TV empire. I wanted to ask if we could talk privately, but I could not bring myself to say the words.

The newsroom was alive with reporters scurrying from phones to typewriters. Jill Redman was coordinating her station's effort at getting the news of the assault to the public. Jill was either ignoring me or was too busy to converse, so I asked a junior reporter from the *Courier* if anyone knew the extent of Commissioner Zachman's injury. He said there were conflicting reports from the county general hospital. One source said George Zachman was conscious but suffering from partial paralysis, and another said he was comatose with a fractured skull.

As the body of people was leaving the chamber, Bart Countryman and Jack Clay pushed their way inward. They showed relief upon seeing me, but concern was still written on their faces.

"Did you witness the fist fight?" Jack asked.

"Yes, I was over there," I said, pointing to the west wall. "The fight was at the council table."

I led them to the platform, where blood and fluid had not as yet been removed. We went over the evident reason for the fight and how close Walter Manville came to being elected the mayor today.

I knew Bart and Jack were going to suggest we

meet with Marcella Baker for a strategy session, but I wished to avoid her since Windy Wetherby unloaded his accusation about her possible tie-up with Al Kelder. If Windy was correct, and it all sounded so logical, I really didn't want to know anymore. Maybe Marcella was in a financial corner and her conscience was clouded for a brief period. Perhaps Kelder took the advantage.

"Let's meet with Marcella," Bart said. "We'll have sufficient time now for reflection on what we've done, what mistakes we've made, what possibility we have of winning and whether the next balloting indeed will be in one week, as Hayden said."

"I must tell you now that it may be best we three meet alone. For two reasons. One, we are seasoned enough to run our own campaign."

"What's the second reason?" Jack Clay asked.

"I'm loathe to give it, but we're all friends here. I trust you two fellows more than anyone else in Burlington. It's just that I don't have facts to justify my reluctance to confer with Marcella."

"What do you mean?" Clay probed.

"I never told you about Windy Wetherby accusing her of having Kelder co-sign her family conglomerate out of bankruptcy. I don't say I believe it, but I didn't want to destroy my good opinion of Marcella, so I didn't delve further for fear I'd find facts to back up Windy's allegation. I hate even to bring it up, because I respect her so much. Her companies were beyond salvation, according to Carter Adams at the Burlington Bank and Trust. There is certainly the possibility, however, that she was given non-collateral backing because of her trustworthiness and prominent name. I don't profess to know the criteria that bankers use in determining which loans are good bets for repayment and which are not."

Jack broke the momentary pause by asking how we should treat Marcella.

"I suppose we owe it to this fine woman and outstanding mayor," I said, "to approach her with Windy's charge. We should let her respond in the most convenient setting possible. This is a high priority item. I probably should be the one to go to Marcella. It could be forgotten except that this cable television intrigue may blow open and expose a lot of people, some of them our supporters. So I guess I'm being selfish by deciding to approach Marcella. But you'll agree, I hope, that it's a wise course to take."

It wasn't clear to Jack how Marcella Baker's resignation could help Al Kelder. I explained the speculation that Kelder wanted Manville in the mayor's office to make certain his company would be given the contract. Walter could sort of be the elected franchise man in residence.

— ★ ★ ★ —

Marcella was back in her office, with an agreement to work half-days. She was shaken by the fight in the council room. Or was it from nearly being found out?

I informed her as gently as I was able about the accusation of Windy Wetherby. She listened without noticeably blinking or flinching. Her eyes were intent and anxious. I felt like the city prosecutor.

"Yes, I heard Al Kelder's offer," Marcella said. "It was at my most desperate moment. I did not say whether I'd accept his help, but he did go to my principal bank where he told an officer he'd provide security for my companies. The bank called and asked if I were going through with Kelder's plan. I told them 'Never.' That's as far as it went."

"In the meantime, I made a decision to do the best I could, but to take whatever consequences that came, without outside help or interference."

"Two things are significant, Connor. First, I made the decision to reject Kelder's help before I decided to resign; and secondly, the impression Kelder gave was that he wanted me to be a legitimate, paid lobbyist for his franchise effort after I was out of office. It wasn't until I had given it some thought that I concluded he had paid someone, probably Walter Manville, a great sum of money to be his employee-mayor. Although I was slow in deducing Kelder's real purpose, I didn't feel I did anything wrong morally."

Reflecting, Marcella said, "It was through Al Kelder that Manville must have found out I would have to resign. That was clever of him to quit before I did."

I was greatly relieved. I warned her she could be subpoenaed to testify eventually about Kelder making a disguised bribe attempt. She said she knew as much and was ready to be a witness against him.

After I left her office, I stopped at St. Catherine's Cathedral to pray for Marcella and the two Republican commissioners. The tumultuous morning caused me to forget that it was Holy Thursday until I saw several lighted confessionals. As I checked a schedule for masses later in the day, I noticed a tiny Mexican-American woman praying aloud near a statue of the Blessed Virgin.

The life-sized marble image depicted a young Mary, no more than eighteen years old. There was a look of serenity on her face as she gazed at the Christ Child. A small curl hung down the forehead of the Babe.

I appealed to the Lady to assist Marcella in her diverse needs. Her marital life surely was crumbling, with her husband's alcoholism and then his failing in business. Then, with Al Kelder trying to taint her, she must have been terribly depressed.

Even though Bert Peterson should not have attacked his partyman, I respected him for his motivation and I asked Mary to intercede on his behalf.

On each of my visits, I asked the Mother of God to open her arms wide for all the unborn babies whose biological mothers decided they should be put to death. I also asked Mary to watch over Ann Marie and her family.

The large cathedral was nearly empty as I knelt at the altar railing to pray to the Blessed Sacrament. I begged mercy for Al Kelder, the shadow man who had nearly wrecked city government. Praying for an enemy or opponent helped remove any bitterness or smallness that I had in my heart.

I hurried as I left the cathedral, realizing I was late for my meeting with Jack Clay and Bart Countryman.

As I drove downtown to the Chaix-Gordon Hotel, I thought that developing a grand strategy from this point forward was going to be difficult since I didn't know if Bert Peterson was going to be charged with assault. If George Zachman had sustained serious injuries, the county attorney likely would take the matter to a grand jury. If it turned out that his injuries were minor, the city attorney, who handled misdemeanors, undoubtedly would prosecute Peterson for simple assault in municipal court. If the claim of Zachman's fractured skull or partial paralysis were true, however, an aggravated assault tag would have to be put on the offense, and that would be a felony, if proven.

I wondered how Bert Peterson could vote for the new mayor, regardless of what was decided by the various prosecutors. It could be argued that he might assault any commissioner voting for a candidate of whom he didn't approve.

If Peterson had any facts to link George Zachman or other council members with bribery, he had a duty to come forward to mitigate the assault and to force an investigation of the cable TV applicants.

Jack and Bart were waiting for me at the curb in front of the hotel, flagging my attention as I approached.

"You can't go in there," Jack said as he opened the passenger door of my car. "You've been discovered. Two *Courier* reporters and all the electronic reporters in town are trying to find you."

"Is it because Pete Holloway pointed me out as being free of any conflicts?"

"Probably in part, but somebody has advanced your name in an impromptu press conference."

My disappointment must have shown. "That would be from Buck Simmons," I said. "We've always been straightforward with each other and I think Buck would like to see me hold higher office than state representative. He knows I'm not a Republican, though. Certainly, he is aware his recommendation will come to a dead end."

"It may not be as noble as it appears," Bart said. "I'll bet he'd do anything to divert the media's focus from the most embarrassing incident his party has suffered locally in decades."

After I repeated the answers Marcella Baker gave me, they jumped into my car and I drove to a delicatessen across the Manitou river.

"Bart and I want you to stay away from the media for a few days or even until balloting resumes," Jack said. "Long enough for the storm to ebb."

We found a table and a waitress brought us coffee. The deli already was filling up for lunch.

"For sure," Jack continued, "we don't want you interviewed about the fight. There is no way you can give the right answers. Reporters are told to put a twist on a story and their adjectives will come out as yours."

"I agree. Being interviewed would somehow make me out to have been a party to the fight."

We spent the next hour trying to formulate a sound plan. Winona Smith was an essential contact. Although she voted for Walter Manville on the last ballot, none of us thought she was party to a bribe. The same with Clark Mathews. He may only have been paying Constance Wetherby back for bringing him into the council. Pete Holloway might be able to work on Sam Talbot; that is, if we can get Holloway's vote. I thought we could count on Pete. Of course, he would serve only as long as George Zachman remained hospitalized. I could not foresee Sonny Wallace or the public-appearing enemies, Wetherby and Hayden, ever coming over to my candidacy. I wouldn't need their votes if Democrats Smith and Talbot, independent Mathews and Republicans Peterson and Holloway voted for me.

We used an assets and liabilities approach to our strategy ideas. The advantages far outweighed the drawbacks in contacting both Bert Peterson and his deputy commissioner, Robb Overstreet, a twenty-three year old in his first year out of college. The liabilities in seeing both men were nebulous.

Bart and Jack had a solid hunch Peterson would continue in his position, but be disqualified from participating in the mayoral balloting because of a court's probation provision. We needed to approach Peterson, regardless, to tell him forthrightly we wanted to meet with his deputy because of our doubts he would be permitted to continue voting. If he were sensitive and refused us, we then could go to Overstreet anyway. Our chance of success with Overstreet would be diminished, though, if we didn't have the commissioner's blessing.

Just as important were the visits with Clark Mathews, Winona Smith and Sam Talbot.

Going through Boss Kane at the Labor Temple to get Talbot's vote held no merit. The Temple would be working hard to advance the name of its endorsee, Vada Griffin. If we could steal Winona from Manville, then Talbot might be convinced to leave the Democrat-labor shackles, as doubtful as that seemed presently. That strategy made Winona the second contact, after Overstreet. Then, Clark Mathews. He was steadfast as Constance Wetherby's mime, but her candidate Walter Manville took a figurative eight-count when his supporter George Zachman took a literal ten-count.

Pete Holloway may be more impressed if we stayed away from him, particularly while his boss was not known to be out of danger.

Sam Talbot was committed to Griffin, so the timing with him was not important.

Bart called the hospital for a report on Zachman's condition. The spokeswoman said a report would be made public in an hour or two. Bart gave her his office number and she promised to phone his secretary when the report was released.

Jack offered to make the initial contact with Bert Peterson while I accompanied Bart to the police headquarters where he could determine Peterson's whereabouts.

XII

The dated, graystone police building was brimming with uniformed personnel. As Bart registered us at the front desk and then went to the second floor to make a private inquiry at Homicide and Assault, four policemen in a semi-circle recognized me.

Drawing me into their conversation, a portly officer asked, "That was a terrible thing that happened, wasn't it?"

I agreed and asked about Zachman's condition.

"We don't know any more than when he was brought into the hospital. He had a convulsion at the emergency entrance. That man lost a lot of blood."

The other officers watched my reaction. I was sincerely sorry Zachman was hurt, but I couldn't feel anger toward Bert Peterson, whose frustration and exasperation carried him into an emotional explosion. I didn't know what I'd have done in a similar setting.

Bart caught up to me as I walked to an elevator. He said his second floor source was either uninformed or close-mouthed about Peterson's whereabouts or fate.

I saw two policemen with their feet propped up on metal desks in the office of the Burglary Division.

A thin, darkhaired sergeant with wire-rimmed glasses sat on the visitors' side of the desk. An older man, also in uniform, twiddled his thumbs. He had a white fringe of hair circling his head horizontally. On his left breast was a badge with the number four on it, the low number presumably signifying longevity. Double bars on his collar indicated captaincy.

"You two look like FBI agents," the younger officer said.

"You're correct," Bart lied. "We're just wondering what caused the fight in the city council."

"Graft caused it," the sergeant said. "Zachman had Al Kelder and Ulric Anderson in a bidding situation and Kelder won. Bert Peterson spent several early-morning hours pleading with Zachman to dissociate himself from the element that had hooked him into it. Obviously, he had no success."

I turned to the captain for corroboration.

"Yes, we know a lot of the background in this whole matter," the senior man said, not under-using the innuendo.

The sergeant was unhappy with himself. He had been open with strangers. Looking at me quizzically and trying to allay his fear, he asked, "Are you really FBI agents?"

"We only look like agents, remember?" Bart answered.

Until then, I couldn't have imagined anonymity ever being helpful to a mayoral candidate.

— ★ ★ ★ —

Carroll Dupre maintained offices in the Midwest Professional Building. It also was where he maintained more than a few broken-down lawyers and out-of-office politicians. He never would let on, however, that he had a social worker's heart.

Carroll was emerging from the building's revolving door as I pushed inward. I swung one hundred and eighty degrees and asked as we met, "Do you still claim no payoffs were made?"

He was friendly, saying, "I think the council just got tired of the jockeying and decided to get it over with. Not a half hour before he was struck, Zachman indicated to me that he'd vote for almost anybody in order to get back to the old routine."

He still was not leveling with me. "I'll have to tell you sometime what your favorite office holder is alleged to have done," I prodded.

He didn't react to the bait except to smile shyly.

As soon as I turned from Dupre and started walking away from the building, Perry Hale, one of the chief authors of the new city charter and a confidante of Commissioner Hayden, passed the main entrance. He was one of the most recent examples of an honest and talented political aide who had turned his back on government work to enter the private sector. Some left for monetary reasons and others because of the insecurity provided by each election, but I believed most departed when they realized their bosses were undedicated hacks not qualified to hold public office.

"Was the loss of the transit commission appointment to his comrade what made Peterson so angry?" I asked Hale.

"I went up to the county attorney's office a few

minutes ago," Hale said, "to find out what had happened."

"What made you think you could find out there?"

"Oh, I anticipated Bert Peterson spilling some facts when he faced questioning by the prosecutors. With public figures, the police usually ask the county attorney to call the person in for an off-the-record discussion of the part played by that person in an incident. A man or woman on the street would not get that treatment, but I know how this city operates."

"So what did you find out?"

"They gave Peterson special consideration, merely requesting that he come in sometime next week. The reason given was that the balloting would not start for one week. So at this time they do not have to accommodate the city council's expected question as to whether Peterson could join in the mayoral voting, regardless of criminal charges or the lack of them. In truth, the county attorney's office also has to research this thing. It could be trampling on Peterson's rights if it denies him the right to vote, and in short, to carry out the duties of his office."

As I was getting to the question of a bribe, a building guard waved a greeting to Hale. I hoped he would not interrupt our conversation and he did not.

"What Ellsworth did today in nominating Constance's candidate was smart politically," Hale said. "When he sees defeat on an issue, he backs off and goes on to the next challenge. I think he saw that he couldn't block Manville, so he took another course, oneupmanship, or in this case, oneupwomanship, if you will. In his eyes, he beat Wetherby by nominating her man. When it came to her vote, she had to cast it for the candidate she had been touting. That made it appear Ellsworth had won. That's all he was interested in."

"Do you infer it was only an ego battle?"

"Yes, I suppose so. Ellsworth tried to salvage some pride."

I couldn't accept the argument that Commissioner Hayden had only ego needs to satisfy. But there was no sense in belaboring it if Hale firmly believed what he was saying, and he has been candid with me in the past.

I had forgotten to thank Hale for answering the technical questions I posed on the days prior to the labor and Democratic screenings. He had told me more extemporaneously about revenue bonds than the entire city council could tell me with preparation. In fact, the only member of the council who had confidence in his own knowledge of funding was Ellsworth Hayden. The others stepped into money matters with painful awareness of their ignorance.

Jack and Bart were to meet me at the Covered Wagon for a late lunch after Jack was to have contacted Bert Peterson.

It was two o'clock when I walked into the Wagon's bar and ordered a drink. I was the only person being served until *Courier* editor Arthur Tanford sauntered up and sighed as he dropped onto an armless stool some ten feet away from me. He took off his sun glasses while his eyes adjusted to the comparative darkness. I could see that the lines in the editor's face had become more prominent. He was looking my way, so we mouthed pleasantries.

Tanford examines topical subjects three times each week in his column. In his most recent denoument, he concluded magnanimously that editorial policy should and does reflect the views of the community. An echo, in other words. If the community wanted genocide, the *Courier* then should editorialize for class killings. And this in fact it did, with editorials favoring murder in the womb for any mother so inclined. He liked to use inane disclaimers, such as, "I wouldn't want my wife or daughter to abort their pregnancies, but if other people wanted to do so, that was their business."

I'll bet his nineteenth century ancestors were known to have said, "I don't keep slaves myself, but if my neighbors want to. . ."

In addition to the poor logic, the *Courier* didn't even echo its readers' views. A recent opinion poll commissioned by the Burlington population assembly, an amalgam of abortion-minded social service agencies, showed local residents to be against induced abortion by a substantial margin. Results of the poll were pirated from one of the agencies and brought to the attention of the *Courier*'s managing editor. Naturally, nothing was printed because the editor was an advocate journalist, not interested in impartiality.

Hundreds of people who labored unceasingly to save fetal life commiserated often over the *Courier*'s abdication of fairness. Week after week, there were quarter-page articles in the inappropriately-named

Family and Wife Section espousing a woman's right to do what she pleased with "her fertilized ovum."

When pro-life women approached the Family and Wife editor to ask for articles outlining the positions and the goals of their movement, the editor ignored them, except to state that the printed media were not governed by the Federal Communications Commission and thus did not have to listen to pleas for fairness. There was no need to be fair when one's newspaper controlled the mass media advertising in town.

As Tanford and I were alone in manning the bar, the urbane master of subtlety wrote feverishly on a notepad provided him by the bartender.

Tanford's name was called out from near the coat check room. It was Percy MacDuff, the man who had outdueled Tanford last year for the job of executive editor. Tanford then gained autonomy on the editorial page and control of the Family and Wife Section, conditions he demanded in agreeing to stay with the *Courier*. Hence, MacDuff could not prevent editorials favoring abortion nor euphemized, advocate articles on the subject by women's page writers who themselves had abortions. He described this plight often to visiting pro-life workers.

The front door of the Covered Wagon was opened forcefully. I expected Bart and Jack, but it was Republican chairman Buck Simmons, who I thought would be in hiding after his party's public fist fight.

He was apprehensive as I motioned him over to the bar. Tanford and MacDuff watched us.

"I've had a hectic few hours, Connor," he said. "Bert Peterson may have wrecked everything that party regulars and I spent years building. There is a good possibility the Republican party in Burlington is finished. Over with. Done!"

If Buck were not such a nice fellow and good friend, I'd have told him there would always be a Republican party as long as there was selfishness. But then, I had no right to injure his feelings; and furthermore, I didn't have a corner on seeing Republicanism objectively.

Just as I was wishing Jack Clay were present to tell how he fared with Peterson, Bart Countryman walked in with Jack right behind him.

Buck was reluctant to get into our strategy talk, but I urged him to stay.

"Commissioner Peterson's going to come out fighting," Jack said, "and he's trying to exact unquestioned loyalty from his deputy."

"Whether or not he fights may make no difference if he's charged with a felony," I said. "Did you get a medical report?"

"It's bad. Zachman still is not conscious and not responding to stimuli. The doctors fear brain damage."

"What did Peterson say about his deputy?"

"He resented my asking and told me to stay away from him."

Assuming Buck Simmons had some official report on Peterson's lot, I asked Buck about the mood at the county attorney's office.

"They have to know whether George has a

serious injury before making a decision. If it's only a punch in the jaw with no residual complications, Bert can be prosecuted for simple assault and fined one hundred dollars. But as long as Zachman remains unconscious, the county attorney will have to be thinking about a felony prosecution."

The discussion turned to the deputy. We didn't want Simmons to anger Burlington Republicans by overtly helping me, so we discouraged him collectively when he offered to contact Robb Overstreet on my behalf. After all, I was a known Democrat and he was the hired Republican chairman, accountable to his myriad employers.

With the mention of Peterson's deputy commissioner, I tried to place myself in Robb's shoes to better understand the decisions he must make. Did he desire a future in politics? Was he an ideological Republican? Rigid in what he believed was a correct course of action, even if he differed with the commissioner? Would he deny a vote to someone he pegged as an eventual opponent for any number of elective or appointive posts? Would his relative youth cause him to act impulsively? Or would his youth allow him more purity in decision-making, letting him see more clearly the insidious encroachment of the Kelder group? Did he influence his boss's indignation and the resulting violence?

All agreed, including Buck Simmons, that once Peterson unequivocally denied Jack permission to meet with his deputy, he opened the door—in a propriety sense—for us to see Overstreet. When we failed by the unwritten but conventional standard, we were freed to do what we believed proper in the first place.

Jack came back from the phone booth quoting the young deputy's secretary as saying he was already incommunicado at an unknown lake cabin.

"I left my name," Jack said, "and a message for him to call me when he gets back in town. I have a hunch that if we don't push too hard for a meeting with Overstreet, the passive effort may have a positive effect. The same with Peter Holloway."

Winona Smith and Clark Mathews, in the predictable order of their coming over to my side, were next on the list of contacts.

We stood at the bar until the genial maitre'd seated us in the less desirable room, which was partioned from the kidney-shaped main dining area by frosted windows. Playfully, we accused the longtime host of saving the tables on the more popular side for his regular customers. As we entered the smaller room, I recognized newly elected Utilities' Commissioner Clark Mathews at a table with his former boss, Walter Manville. The dimness of the room's light prevented me from identifying the third man, although I could see that he had thick, dark hair and a crooked nose.

I said hello to both Mathews and Manville as Bart and Jack led the way to a table. Manville did not return my greeting, but the surprised Mathews winked at me, speaking resonantly, "Well, how do you do, candidate?"

As I slid into a captain's chair, I observed that the third person was none other than Democratic

Congressman Cortland Peabody. I flushed momentarily. It was as if a partially clarifying scent wafted past my nostrils. Still, the revelation was only a blur.

If my eyes hadn't seen it, I would have claimed the specter of Peabody sitting down to lunch with Manville and Mathews was improbable if not impossible.

Peabody represented a hard-hat district for a few months short of thirty years. For the past ten years, there were recurring rumors of his retirement. Every election year, prospective candidates made noises around the district for a few weeks, disappearing when the rumors proved erroneous. The congressional district encompassed only one moderately prosperous section of Burlington, and that was where the congressman, Manville and I maintained residences, all within three blocks of each other.

With Congressman Peabody a labor Democrat and Manville an independent and closet Republican, it was difficult to imagine what they had to discuss in a secluded setting such as the darkened dining room. There was at least one connection, though. The congressman seemed to come home from Washington almost every weekend. Stewardesses reported quietly to Republican headquarters that two men always met him at the airport and handed him money, possibly a total each time of ten or twelve hundred dollars in one hundred dollar denominations. Buck wouldn't discuss it with me, but I learned that the gift-bearers were from diverse backgrounds. One was head of a union; which one I didn't know. The other was a junior executive of the Paragon Plastics Company, a Burlington concern that did a great amount of government contract work and had Walter Manville sitting on its board of directors.

I felt this last was the force bringing Peabody and Manville to their murky rendezvous, and not the prospect of Manville succeeding the elderly congressman in the fall if he won the present mayoral contest.

There was one other tie the men had. Both were pro-abortion. For that reason, I could understand Peabody wanting Manville in congress at a time the Human Life Amendment to the constitution came up for a floor vote. But I couldn't visualize Manville trying to capture one of the most secured labor districts in the entire House of Representatives.

I had never heard Cortland Peabody's name used in concert with the cable TV matter, so I had no reason to believe he was Al Kelder's Washington connection.

As we tried to unravel the strange mix of politicians at the nearby table, Commissioner Wetherby's deputy, Lainy Ross, materialized through the door near the kitchen. I didn't think she saw Manville and his party and they didn't notice her. We invited her to sit with us and Bart helped her into a chair.

"I've been searching for you," Lainy said. "One of the city or county prosecutors had a session with an unidentified judge and Commissioner Peterson a few minutes ago. The prosecutor offered to let Peterson plead guilty to simple assault. Peterson accepted quickly and the judge fined him twenty-five dollars with no mention of probation."

Lainy was beginning to talk loudly enough so that Manville's group became quiet. After I whispered the identity of the other table's occupants, Lainy continued in a subdued voice. She said she had resigned as deputy commissioner an hour earlier because of Constance Wetherby's progressive involvement with the TV combine. Feeling Winona Smith was naive about the Kelder manipulations, Lainy went to Winona as soon as she was free of Constance, and she discussed with Winona the possible reasons for each commissioner's mayoral vote.

Lainy couldn't be certain Winona's ignorance was genuine or feigned. She thought back to the time several commissioners received cars and boats and wondered if Winona had been one of those.

"Even if she were," Lainy said, "I don't believe Winona is crafty enough to know what is going on. I told her from here on in, I was supporting your candidacy, Connor, and I suggested she take some time and ponder the fact that nobody owns you. In short, I asked for her vote. She promised not to rule you out at an early date. That's the best I could do."

We thanked Lainy in unison as Sonny Wallace sat down at the table with Walter Manville, Clark Mathews and Congressman Cortland Peabody.

Buck Simmons came into the room from the bar with a drink in hand. I lifted a chair from another table as Lainy filled Buck in on her resignation, on the special treatment accorded Peterson, and on Winona Smith's reaction or lack of it.

While Lainy spoke, Buck stared at the sharers of the other table. Sonny Wallace was talking guardedly; and then, abruptly and synchronously, his group stood and disappeared from the room through the far exit.

Mathews, the follower, waved to us covertly as he tripped along at the rear of the strange bedfellows.

Suddenly, Sam Talbot became the swing vote. Clark Mathews's gesture told us he was a possibility. The basic honesty of Winona Smith made her a doubtful participant in the television conspiracy, and therefore a potential ally. If Pete Holloway and Robb Overstreet were made acting commissioners, we could have a chance with both of them. And then Sam Talbot could be my fifth vote. There was no likelihood of my getting the votes of Wetherby, Hayden and Wallace.

Even though I was no more certain of one, two or five votes, it was satisfying to have the task ahead delineated as clearly as it was now.

It was agreed Winona and Clark must be contacted early and Robb and Pete left alone for a few days. As for Talbot, our swing vote hopeful, we did not reach a consensus on the way to capture him.

I had a feeling Clark Mathews might slip and unload some secrets about the purpose of his clique's meeting, wherever it met after our presence impeded its progress at the Covered Wagon.

Bart and Jack would try to arrange an appointment with Mathews. Lainy indicated that she would be out of town until Easter Sunday.

For my part, I was going to Holy Thursday mass. My need was great for a spiritual respite from the manipulations of Al Kelder.

— ★ ★ ★ —

The Last Supper day always was pleasurable for me despite the ominous cloud of Calvary casting a shadow over the ceremonies which commemorate the institution of both the Eucharist and the priesthood.

St. Catherine's Cathedral was full of worshippers when I arrived for the five o'clock afternoon mass. As I genuflected and knelt next to a wizened little woman whose scarf covered the contours of her weathered profile, someone pushed a finger into my back. Turning, I saw a beaming Marny Mathews, wife of Clark. She was alone. A recent convert to Catholicism, Marny was unabashed in her devotion to the church.

"Wait for me after mass," she insisted.

In a moving homily, the celebrant spoke of the new commandment that Jesus gave on his last Thursday on earth: "That as I have loved you, you also love one another. By this all will know that you are my disciples, if you have love for one another."

Before celebrating the Eucharist, the priest, reenacting the scene in the upper room, washed the feet of twelve of the laity.

Since I always had felt more comfortable making prayerful requests when they were coupled with equal expressions of thanksgiving, I thanked Jesus for Mayor Baker's non-involvement with Al Kelder before I asked for the realization of Marny's and Clark's dreams, whatever they were.

Lithesome Marny placed her hand inside my arm as we inched out of the cathedral with the rest of the congregation. She smiled the smile of the good news' bearer.

In the church vestibule, still holding my arm, she said, "Clark and I don't have many secrets, Connor. I'm aware of the cable TV payoffs and most of the backroom moves." She stopped, glancing at me until she was certain I comprehended her subject.

"Clark wanted me to urge that you remain in the race. He thought I'd see you at mass. Clark doesn't know about the other council members right now, but as for himself, he said that there was a chance he may vote for you. That's as much as he can say now."

Although his furtive wave at the Covered Wagon told me that his vote was possible, I was pleased when Marny confirmed it.

— ★ ★ ★ —

I ate a quiet dinner at DiNapoli's, an Italian restaurant set above Norway pine trees on a hillside south of the city. Normally busy on week nights as well as weekends, the DiNapoli had few diners this evening. All of the booths and tables were situated along four terraces, providing window seats for customers to view arriving and departing planes at the Burlington airport.

The sky was dark. Brilliant hues of red and green and blue lights outlined the landing strips and taxiing aprons.

Proprietor Mama Martino sat for awhile with me. We sipped a dark red wine and exchanged toasts after which I ate too much lasagne. Mama generally stuffed a lot of beef among the noodles, causing me to forget my capacity. For a few pacific moments, I was not preoccupied with the day's explosive event or the delicate work ahead.

I was being recognized more often by the public since my picture had appeared in three straight editions of the *Courier*. When I signaled for my bill, the waiter announced that an older couple sitting in a top-terrace booth already had paid my check and left the restaurant without giving their names.

By custom, the Blessed Sacrament was exposed until midnight on Holy Thursday for adoration by the faithful, but the little chapel I stopped at was locked when I tried the door.

Restive, I continued down London Road to the old warehouse where I had seen Polly Lanier, the secretary of Ellsworth Hayden. I knew in my psyche that the warehouse held some answer to the speculation of graft at City Hall. If I only had more time, I could wade through the corporate subterfuges that surely must exist for the purpose of clouding the building's ownership.

Whom could I call at this eleventh hour with some knowledge of abstract properties? A title lawyer would be the ideal person, but I needed someone who could lay aside all other tasks tomorrow morning to make a whirlwind attempt at finding the warehouse's title chronology. Even if it were traced forward to a dummy corporation, it still would be headway and it could portend the next step.

When temporary mayor Hayden had proclaimed the interruption of balloting and council meetings, I doubted its legality, as the charter called for city council meetings on each weekday. Therefore, if he had a selfish reason for wanting to change the date balloting would resume, I believed that all he had to do was publicize it. With that in mind, I had to be ready to produce votes Monday morning. And that made Friday the last day I had to dig into county records.

The only person I could conceive of with expertise and trustworthiness and the time to do the work was one whose support could lie with another candidate. But Allison Reynolds accepted immediately the assignment which I outlined on the telephone. She called me at my home an hour later with several thorough questions on points I had only outlined in our earlier conversation.

The wife of lawyer-industrialist Courtney Reynolds really was turned on. I knew when I was screened by the Democratic committee that Allison was a strong-minded member whose ire I did not want to trigger. Now her strength and dedication to principle were being put to work for my benefit. This pleased me and I told her so as we agreed to an investigative course before saying good night.

XIII

Awakening early on Good Friday morning, I was determined to ascertain the true ownership of the warehouse or else get off the smell of collusion and return to a more positive campaign road.

As Allison had requested, I called to tell her where to meet me so that we could jot down license numbers at the warehouse and then go in my car to the motor vehicle headquarters to establish ownership of the cars. There was no response to the jarring ring of the telephone. It was too early to call the office of Allison's husband to find out where she was, so I got into my car and headed onto London Road, thinking she misunderstood the instruction to await my phone call.

Parking was prohibited on weekday mornings from seven to nine in front of the warehouse, so I steered toward an alley and pulled into a parking lot at the rear of the building. I didn't recognize any of the six parked cars, but I identified immediately the bushy blond head of Sonny Wallace. He was sitting with his back against shelves of books and his profile showed through a large floor-length window at the rear of the structure. A modern board room table was evident, too, with people gesticulating on both sides. No attention was diverted to the parking lot.

I would have been noticed if I waited for Allison, so I wrote down as many license numbers as I could in a few seconds, from one vantage point. Then I drove out of the alley and stopped at a pay telephone booth. Again, there was no answer at the Reynolds house.

Becoming concerned, I accelerated in the direction of her street. I had no plan, but her absence mystified me so much that I decided to find out whether her telephone was out of order.

I pushed the metal button and knocked on the outer door. A black Labrador dog bared its teeth as it pawed a window panel at the side of the front door. As I heard the graduating melody of the door chimes, I backed up to appraise the splendor of the Reynolds' Tudor mansion. For a moment, I thought I saw a face behind an upstairs curtain. There seemed to be no movement downstairs. It already was eight o'clock, so Allison's children probably were on their way to school. Still, the couple must have had a full-time maid or perhaps even a gardener. "Where were they?" I wondered.

The frustrating thing was that I was wasting irreplaceable time. At first, I worried that Allison would be somewhere remonstrating with me in absentia because I wasn't at some prearranged spot. As the minutes elapsed, though, I began to think that she had misgivings about her role.

Maybe Allison thought first with her emotions, and then, as the possible consequences sank into her head, her thinking processes outvoted her feelings.

I could have called Courtney Reynolds's law

office, but since I was intending to head in that direction anyway, I turned onto London Road and drove downtown. Parking in an inside ramp, I took an elevator to the penthouse floor that Courtney shared with two other businessmen-lawyers.

Though it was only eight-forty, I counted on Courtney being at his office after the family telephone and doorbell went unanswered.

A stylishly dressed receptionist in her late thirties told me that she didn't think he would be coming in. "The family undoubtedly will be spending a long weekend at its resort home north of Burlington. Could I have your name so that Mr. Reynolds can call you on Monday?"

While I fenced with her in an attempt to remain anonymous, Courtney Reynolds appeared suddenly, crossing the room in the midst of a secretarial pool behind the reception desk. Both the receptionist and I flinched, she with embarrassment, I with irritation. "Are you sure he won't be in today?" I asked sarcastically, blaming the conduit for following instructions.

Courtney saw me. He walked directly to the hallway leading to private offices and motioned for me to follow him. We passed several ornately framed portraits, presumably of his pioneering ancestors.

"Allison is here," he said in an aside as he opened the oaken door to his grandly appointed office. There were two leather sofas, a conference table, a mahogany table-desk and picture windows on adjoining walls.

The set-jaw look on Allison's face told me they had argued. She smiled wanly as I said my greeting.

Courtney was candid. He admitted they had quarreled over Allison's eagerness to assist me.

Standing in front of me with a pleading motion, Courtney said, "I would have no objection to Allison's involvement in this title search except for one fear I have. If organized crime is behind any payola which certain commissioners are said to be discovering in their accounts, then there is the possibility of violence facing anyone trying to block the process. With that being a real and immediate danger, I cannot allow my wife to help you. It's that simple. I like what you're doing, but I am not going to take the chance of Allison being hurt."

There could be no rebuttal to his reasoning. I felt uneasy, having been the cause of the couple's disagreement. Thanking Courtney for his sincerity and Allison for her intended help, I departed as tactfully as I could.

In one sense, it was a relief. I had never been very comfortable with the wealthy, regardless of the conditions. Their usual method of judging people was by the amount of money they made. Employees were mere tools to fatten holdings. Condescension and a demanding attitude were justified. Poverty was not linked to a dearth of talent, a broken home or a lack of capital, but was caused by indolence, a conclusion undoubtedly reached at such industrious places as Aspen, Palm Springs or Acapulco. The mentality pattern was the same in every city's Main Line.

I must surely be an unchristian ingrate. Here, Allison and Courtney treated me kindly and civilly and I categorized them with heartless and avaricious snobs!

— ★ ★ ★ —

At nine o'clock on Good Friday morning I hadn't started the job of tracking the warehouse owners. Phone calls had kept me busy. Municipal offices would close at noon, so I would have to hurry.

Now I was on my own again. There was not enough time to brief Jack, Lainy or Bart on my sleuthing need. I'd just have to feel my way along, unschooled in the procedures and shortcuts in determining property ownership.

But I did think I knew how to check automobile ownership, until a clerk at the Motor Vehicle registration center caught me off guard.

"Why do you want this information?" she asked.

"Do I need a reason? Aren't these public records?"

"Yes, but we like to know who we're dealing with and why the license identification is sought. You have to understand, sir, that there are a lot of kooky people trying to find home addresses of women through their automobile license numbers."

I told her I was sorry and said I wanted only to ascertain whether the tenants of a certain building were using its parking lot. That satisfied her and she went to a computer console and began to feed it with information. I was lucky. If she had said I could come back on Monday and speak with her boss, I'd have been in fine shape.

I hoped she would take the printout from the computer and hand it to me without reading the names, but she scanned the paper as she returned to the counter.

Thinking there was a mistake, she said, "Most of these people are politicians, aren't they? I thought you wanted tenants' names?"

I hadn't been very fair with her, so I gave her an insight into my purpose: "I'm trying to find the real owners of the building where the cars were parked. I can't tell you anything more."

She was not interested. Thankfully.

As soon as I was outside the registration center, I opened the folded printout. There were five vehicle listings: Constance Wetherby, Ellsworth Hayden, Walter Manville and then two cars registered to Lakeside Marine. I definitely had seen Sonny Wallace's head at the large rear window of the building, so he must have been a passenger in one of the cars. Al Kelder apparently had been in one of the Lakeside Marine cars, and if I took a guess, I'd say Congressman Peabody had been driven there by a Lakeside employee. Bert Peterson, and George Zachman or their deputies, Winona Smith and the man we had to extricate from the labor fold—Sam Talbot—probably had not been at the warehouse this morning.

There were no surprises, but the information did serve as a confirmation of my previous suspicions. City council members undoubtedly had been snared by Kelder for their franchise votes alone. But Cortland Peabody, if he were involved, would fit into the group by acting as Kelder's congressional protection against the Federal Communications Commission. The prices had to be high, but even so, I could not imagine Peabody taking the chance of an entanglement with a group, where the propensity for secret-leaking would be greater than with one person. If everyone was in it together, however, each had something on the other and that in itself should seal all of the tongues.

The only way to uncover the bribe payments, then, was to obtain records of transactions, the very method Kelder must have employed to guarantee that promises of favorable votes would be kept. It was for that reason I thought Courtney Reynolds was wrong in suggesting that organized crime was tied to the scheme. Mobsters could pay with cash and enforce promises of votes with threats of violence, if necessary. Because Kelder evidently resorted to traceable payments, I doubted he was associated with national crime figures.

— ★ ★ ★ —

I would not be astonished to find Al Kelder's name at the abstract office as the onetime but not most recent (publicly recorded) owner of the warehouse. The building was in the commercial section of town where he supposedly owned properties that were to be leveled for urban renewal projects.

I called the city engineer's office and gave the address of 1230 North London Road. "I'd like to have a legal description of the property and I was informed your office was the place to get it."

I was referred to the public works' department,

where I did not expect to find "legals".

A woman with a gravely voice said, "For legal purposes, 1230 North London Road is the north ninety feet of lot two and the south ninety feet of the east half of lot one of block twelve, Cummins Industrial Park, Jackson County. For ownership information, you will have to call the county auditor."

The auditor's office reported that Hartford Investment Company owned the building. The subterfuge came sooner than I had expected. The woman suggested phoning the Pioneer Abstract Company to see if there was a registered contract-for-deed.

There, a clerk reiterated that Hartford was the owner and there was no registered contract. Hartford was the apparent straw man. "The last purchase date," she said, "was nine years ago, May seventeenth."

I had to determine whether Hartford was the facade owner, possibly holding an unregistered contract. But before I called or did any more leg work, it would be worthwhile, I felt, to contact the last previous owner to ask the name of the individual at Hartford Investment Company who acted on behalf of the company. First, I telephoned the Secretary of State's office to gain the names of the corporate officers of Hartford. None sounded familiar when they were read to me. Kelder's name was not mentioned.

Back to Pioneer Abstract. "I forgot to ask you for the name of the owner prior to Hartford Investment. That was the property out on London Road." I thought I had the same person I had spoken with previously. "While you're at it, can you tell me if there's an individual's name on the transfer to Hartford?"

"I'll see."

After a minute or two, the clerk came back to the phone and said, "It looks as if the Valley Savings and Loan was the previous registered owner, again with no contract registered to a second party. The person representing Hartford was A. C. Wollkelder. You know who that is, don't you?"

I confessed that I did not.

"Wollkelder was an old country name. The story told is that it was an upper class family in Birmingham, England, until something disgraceful happened. The members scattered, with A. C. Wollkelder settling in Burlington and eventually shortening his name to Kelder."

"Oh, my gosh!"

"You're Representative Mullaney, aren't you?"

"Yes, with whom am I speaking?"

"My name is Grace Warren. We aren't acquainted. I heard you on the ten o'clock news last evening and I thought I recognized your voice now. There are a lot of us at Pioneer Abstract hoping you'll win. Some of us may be able to help you verify the bribery rumors, so let me know if I can document anything further for you."

I told her how much I appreciated her offer of assistance, but I suggested she likely would be stymied, with the true owners probably hidden in unregistered contracts-for-deed.

A woman at the County Revenue Department said the taxes on the warehouse were paid by Hartford Investment. As she spoke, a voice in the background said, "They must have it unregistered." With that information, the clerk paused, then continued: "Hartford Investment is the fee owner and A. Kelder the transfer owner." I didn't know what that meant and I wasn't even certain I heard her correctly.

I considered myself at the end of the information line. Even if I knew someone at Hartford Investment Company, that person wasn't likely to know of a new and unregistered contract. Those things were held in safe deposit boxes, not in file cabinets.

I had been successful in finding Al Kelder's name associated with the masked owner of the warehouse, but unless I received a tip from a Hartford employee or obtained a copy of the unregistered deed, the only other way I knew of to learn the true owners' names was to see personal tax records for property tax payments, or Hartford bank deposit records for tax remittances from the real owners. If the ownership change had been made recently, though, payments would not be made by the new owners for at least several months, unless back taxes were due.

When I checked on the current corporate officers of Hartford at the Secretary of State's office, I should have asked for the names of the original officers and any subsequent changes. It was a few minutes before noon, so I was out of luck until Monday because state offices would be closing for the Three Hours.

XIV

Sᴇᴠᴇɴ ᴏꜰ ᴛʜᴇ Stations on the Via Dolorosa at St. John Vianney Seminary were on the south edge of a creekbed. The other seven were on an elevated walkway on the north bank.

In wending through the cedar trees along the glazed brook, I was fulfilling a wish I had had for years to pray and contemplate the divine death away from a formalized observation.

I must have indicated to Bart Countryman and Lainy Ross where I'd be this afternoon because I could see them standing on the high bank next to the Fourteenth Station. Bart saw me studying them, so I pointed to myself and then to them as if to ask whether there was an urgency in their need to talk with me. He shook his head horizontally, so I went on from the Fourth Station, where Jesus met his afflicted mother, to the Fifth Station, where Simon of Cyrene helped Jesus carry his cross.

I felt myself hurrying as I prayed the Sixth and Seventh Stations and traversed the brook on a foot bridge to the Eighth Station at the top of several unsecured stone steps.

Some of the seminarians were starting to file down a knoll toward the First Station. They seemed to walk in preoccupation.

DECISION AT BURLINGTON

The Eleventh Station. Jesus was nailed to the cross. I stayed kneeling there, recalling where Jesus's pain had been great, and I closed my eyes as I apologized for all the times my thoughts and actions had facilitated the crucifiers.

The Twelfth Station. Jesus died on the cross. I beckoned to Lainey and Bart to join me at the huge carving depicting the expired Savior.

On the last two stations, the body of Jesus was taken down from the cross and placed in the sepulchre.

Bart suggested we weren't in such a hurry that we couldn't take turns reading the passion. I agreed, so we chose a park bench on the seminary's sloping lawn, far enough from the students so as not to disturb them.

Sitting outside on this chilled anniversary of the deicide, thoughts of my battle for the mayor's office diminished in significance, helping to dispel the anxiety that had gripped me this past week.

Reading of the betrayal and poltroonery, the nonfeasance of Pilate, the anguish of Mary and the women of Jerusalem, and the monstrous cruelty of the cross, we inept imitators of the Messiah were sober and quiet as we ambled to my car, where I opened the passenger door for Lainy.

"We've been making contacts," Lainy said. "Robb Overstreet wants to meet briefly with you tonight. He emphasized that Bart, Jack and I can be present, but he does want to meet with you personally. I was sure you had nothing planned tonight, so I arranged a nine-thirty conference at the DiNapoli restaurant."

"As important as it is, Lainy," I interrupted, "please call Overstreet and ask if we can see him tomorrow morning. I don't want a lot of political activity on Good Friday."

"Let's exchange what information we have," I continued, "and then part until tomorrow. Overstreet doesn't seem to be the type to demand something in return for his vote, so I have to believe that he wants a vis-a-vis meeting to give me some bad news firsthand."

Bart blew out a match after lighting a cigar taken from a silver cylinder. "Winona's definitely out of town," he reported, "but she may be back before Sunday, according to her son."

"Hey, where's Jack Clay?" I asked.

"He's trying to find George Zachman's deputy," Lainy said. "We've heard rumblings that Ellsworth Hayden is going to call for more mayoral ballots on Monday, this after his requesting a motion for a week's postponement of city council meetings. With this possibility, we decided to be more forward with Pete Holloway. If Jack can get a promise of Pete's vote, then we can go on to another commissioner. Maybe it will backfire when we assert ourselves, but we have decided to make our move."

I filled them in on my finding Al Kelder's name associated with the sale of the warehouse nine years ago, and of the inconclusive result of the search for current owners' names.

"That must be the reason Allison Reynolds is trying to find you," Bart said. "I didn't tell her you'd be out here this afternoon."

"I'll call her in the morning. She's probably only curious to know whether I connected any city council members' names with Kelder on the warehouse ownership."

"She didn't mention anything else, so I suppose you're right."

"Well, I'll call her. Where do we stand with Sam Talbot? Is he locked inexorably to Vada Griffin, or at least to the Labor Temple?"

"He hasn't been interested enough to make more than monosyllabic grunts to us," Lainy complained. "His campaign funds, his blockworkers, and all those thousands of labor votes in next fall's general election will keep him from coming to our side. The ironic part is that you're a friend of labor and that body has done nothing but hurt your candidacy."

Lainy questioned the wisdom of chasing Sam Talbot when we didn't know if Bert Peterson and George Zachman would be disqualified. "And how will the deputies vote if they assume their bosses' seats?" she asked.

Bart asked if I agreed to chart a more aggressive pursuit of Holloway. I told him to do what he thought was best. On some of those points, hunches changed from hour to hour. We just had to play them as they appeared at the time they surfaced. I thought it was a mistake to be apprehensive, so I was pleased he wanted to push ahead.

Lainy and Bart were impressed with the story I told of Marny Mathews giving me half a promise of Clark's vote when we met last night at the cathedral.

The part that suited all of us was to put our effort into solidifying four of eight votes rather than concentrating on Talbot or one of the Kelder indenturees. Bart would stay close to Winona Smith's house and have a soul session as soon as she was back in Burlington. Lainy would line up a meeting with Robb Overstreet tomorrow. Jack would try to hang a little persuasion on Pete Holloway and I was going to let Marny's friendliness at mass be my invitation to a talk with Clark. After his Freudian greeting yesterday at lunch, I really didn't need a door opener. . .I hoped.

Allison Reynolds was sitting on my front step as I turned into the driveway next to my apartment building.

"Where have you been? I've covered this city looking for you."

She wasn't angry, only concerned that I had gotten too close to the Kelder secrets.

"Courtney and I have been attempting to buy the warehouse. I don't know the result of your digging, if you did do any, but I was sure you would run into a dead end; so Courtney and I decided we'd never be able to live with ourselves if we didn't accept your request for help."

Allison was gesturing wildly as she related how her husband approached Constance Wetherby and Sonny Wallace and inquired how much they wanted for their shares of the warehouse. He said he needed the space for an import company supply center he acquired recently."

"You and Courtney did this for me?" I asked

incredulously.

Here was a very rich man laying safety aside to help me when we were not well acquainted. Allison's participation didn't surprise me, though.

"We did it for you, but also for ourselves. We were part of the crowd who griped bitterly about the Watergate immorality but who contributed nothing to politics and prospective officeholders; not money, time or skill; except for my membership on the screening committee."

"This was one way we felt we could serve you and the cause of better government. Sounds lofty and schmaltzy, but you know there will be more Watergates if the electorate does not immerse itself in the campaigns of straight candidates."

"I know. I know."

"Courtney and I picked up a commercial realtor and drove around the warehouse. The realtor said he had an industrial client recently who placed a million dollar value on the building. He thought it was worth about two or three hundred thousand less than that. Since there wasn't ample time and because we didn't want to involve the realtor in a brazen attempt at extracting from city council members some ownership verification, Courtney decided to take the bold step of a direct contact. He could produce likely credentials showing he was a legitimate prospect for purchasing the warehouse, and then, none of the commissioners knew of his interest in your candidacy."

"When he met with Wetherby and Wallace, Sonny shot some daggers at Courtney with his big blue eyes, but he remained quiet. Constance tried to play the dumb role too convincingly, Courtney thought."

"Later, when Courtney got back to his office, there was a message to contact Constance. Before he called her, he set up a tape system to his telephone to record their conversation. Constance is well-known for disavowing statements she makes and secret meetings she attends."

Allison quickly added that only when a third party and non-participant recorded a conversation did it become illegal wiretapping.

"I heard the tape," she said. "Constance asked first how Courtney found out about the transfer of ownership. He said he stumbled onto it, which wasn't far from the truth. Then, Constance cautiously but gullibly inquired about the amount Courtney would be willing to pay for her share of the building."

"Courtney told her the realtor thought it might be worth about seven hundred thousand. He then had a reason to ask Constance, 'How can I place a valuation on your share when I don't know how many people are owners of the property?' That was when she said there were six equal owners. Then Courtney drove in his next wedge: 'My offer would be contingent on my buying the whole building. Do you think the other owners would be willing to sell? Can you give me their names?' Constance hesitated, saying, 'I'd better talk it over with the others before giving you an answer.' "

"The other owners wouldn't be as open as Commissioner Wetherby, so Courtney became brave. He asked, 'Do you think Hayden, Wallace, Zachman, Manville and Congressman Peabody would object if I called and asked them what their price is?' I liked the way Courtney put that last line: '. . .what their price is.' Yes, I liked that," Allison repeated, grinning.

"Constance fell into the trap Courtney set to get a direct acknowledgement of Sonny Wallace's shareholding. She said, 'You already asked Sonny what his price was and he didn't answer you.' The tape had it perfectly," Allison said. "Mrs. Wetherby didn't seem to show any suspicion. She informed Courtney he'd have to ask those he named what their prices were. In keeping with her initial boldness, she offered her share at two hundred and fifty thousand, or one-sixth of a million and a half. This was more than double the package figure Courtney had mentioned. He didn't argue with the amount, nor did he tell Constance he'd pay one cent for her share. He had what he wanted and didn't try to overplay his position."

I told Allison it was a tremendous coup, while wondering aloud if Courtney had changed his feeling about the possibility of danger.

"We discussed that at length," Allison said. "Courtney is very painstaking. He went over every angle before he was convinced Al Kelder was not connected nationally with a crime syndicate. That gave us the confidence to move forward. Because of our personal friendship with the police chief and his wife, Courtney gave the chief an idea of what he was doing and why he was doing it."

"The police chief said he would have our house watched and our cars tailed on the condition that the tape was taken to the city prosecutor. This answered the dilemma we had about what to do with the tape. Courtney met with the first assistant city prosecutor and the two went through the transcription, detail by detail, covering the ramifications and possible statutes that might apply. Courtney said the prosecutor was debating whether to call in Commissioners Wetherby and Wallace and play the tape back to them."

It sounded like roses for me, even if I usually doubted political advances until the proof was staring at me. I had wanted to lead the Burlington electorate with a positive, forward-thinking, issue-oriented campaign. But this was an eight-voter election where the small electorate was not interested in the issues or in a positive, forward-thinking campaign. Maybe it respected only negative power, such as that provided by Courtney and Allison. I was overwhelmed by their acts of courage, of their commitment to my candidacy. I put an arm around beautiful Allison and asked her to get Courtney and come back to my place. She insisted we go to their estate where their maid could prepare a meatless meal while we had time to recapitulate our separate findings.

I showered and changed into fresh clothes before driving to the Reynolds mansion where the couple's eldest daughter greeted me.

In keeping with the solemnity of the day, our partying was low-keyed. I toasted Courtney's and

Allison's intrepidity as they wished me success when the balloting commenced next week.

We closed the evening on a serious note after noticing a darkened squad car in the alley behind their long, manicured lawn, and an unmarked patrol car with parking lights on, sitting next to a semi-circle driveway at the front of their property.

XV

The saturday morning *Courier* broke its recent editorial silence rather abruptly:

With the nearly unprecedented intramural election for the office of mayor in Burlington, this newspaper's editorial staff agonized this past week before agreeing to endorse a candidate. In an at-large election in which all of the city's voters participate, the *Courier* has a responsibility to indicate its preference. But with eight mortal commissioners choosing their leader, there is the prospect that an endorsement could be an undue influence on those eight voters, who possess frightening power in this case.

The conclusion finally was reached, however, that a sub-surface issue loomed too importantly to let pass without editorial comment. The right to terminate a pregnancy is the issue at stake.

The *Courier* learned Friday of the impending retirement of Congressman Cortland Peabody. Since part of Burlington lies within Peabody's congressional district, the city's mayor automatically will be a favorite in this November's non-incumbent congressional election, if he chooses to graduate to that race. In the present situation, it is a virtual certainty. Reliable sources have stated that both Walter Manville and Connor Mullaney, leading candidates for the mayor's office, and both residing in Peabody's district, are aiming higher than the city post.

Manville takes a moderate position on the right to end a pregnancy, while Mullaney seems to expostulate with reformers on each level of change produced by responsible groups, ranging from the local feminist abortion league to the United States Supreme Court.

Both men come from impressive governmental backgrounds, but we believe the person elected mayor will be casting a vote in congress for or against the so-called Human Life Amendment, which provides for the protection of life at every stage of its biological development. This is too great an issue for the *Courier* to remain quiet. Indeed, to do so would be an abdication by this newspaper of its civic and social responsibility to defend the right to privacy of over fifty per cent of our populace—our women—when they decide whether or not to remove the products of conception from their wombs.

We get impatient with pro-life advocates when they compare abortion to class killings of Jews at extermination camps. Nor do we think a private decision at eight months' gestation is the same as killing a one week old baby, although we are sympathetic to the latter if the baby is defective, and hence a burden to society.

In this enlightened and liberated period, let us not regress to the slavery in which women found themselves in all of previous history. A vote for Connor Mullaney would stunt the progress already made.

If I were in an at-large election, the editorial would hurt me, stupid as it was. But this would be an expression of choice by eight persons whose thoughts were not known to be on the right of the conceived to life nor on the right of those born to kill the conceived.

I must have slept through the ringing of my doorbell. A note was pinned to the outer door from Jack Clay telling me Robb Overstreet would join our group at the DiNapoli Restaurant at one-thirty for a late lunch. The timing would favor me. I wanted to meet this morning with the city finance department's chief accountant to go over two sections of the budget that his office had been so critical of lately.

It was a fruitful conference. The chief accounting officer for the past twenty-seven years told me it was the first time in his memory that the State Public Examiner questioned him about the expense accounts of five members of the city council. It seemed Ellsworth Hayden, Sonny Wallace, Constance Wetherby, George Zachman and former Commissioner Walter Manville each made three trips to Washington, D.C. in the past two weeks. The stated reason each traveler gave for the trips was "Federal Funding for Cities" but a check by the Public Examiner revealed that none of the committee members in charge of federal disbursement to cities had been contacted by city council members. An investigation now was under way to determine where the commissioners actually had spent their time while in Washington. I suggested to the accounting head that he start with Congressman Peabody's office and work his way to the various House and Senate members responsible for striking down stiff regulatory legislation proposed for cable TV companies.

The traveling salesmen's roundtable at the Di Napoli was occupied by Bart, Lainy, Jack, Robb Overstreet and one person I hadn't planned on: Pete Holloway.

When I ensconced myself on a comfortable red leather throne chair, everyone at the table looked to Jack Clay to speak.

"The hospital issued a statement this morning on George Zachman's condition," Jack said. "He is conscious now, but he has a fractured skull and will be a bed patient for awhile. I also found out that the judge who convicted Bert Peterson made him promise he would suspend himself without pay for one month and would make a public apology to Commissioner Zachman."

Pausing, Jack continued, "Now the Republican party has requested, demanded really, that the deputies come down with a bad case of the flu until the balloting is over and a new mayor is selected. Their rationale is that the party has suffered enough embarrassment, not only because of the fight, but also due to some of the voting differences of Zachman and Peterson. Then, when Pete cast his vote for Ma Hayden, party officers were incensed. Rather bluntly, they informed Pete and Robb that future endorsements by the Republican party would depend on whether or not they cast votes in this election.

The deputies were studying me intently as I swung my view around the table.

"What did you fellows tell them?" I asked.

"I was against it from the start," Robb said, "and

I let party officers know this at a wide-open, informal meeting we held. I actually think some of them were pleased. As for Pete, I believe he favored the idea at first. You go ahead and tell Connor, Pete."

"I had three or four motivations pushing me in separate directions. There were those who said I had a bright future in the Republican family, but some of the most solid party people intimated later that the bright future might best be guaranteed by the opposite of that which was being thrust on us by those in power. One of the other forces within me said I should simply do what I thought was proper and correct. Then, my supporters prevailed upon me to be less contrary to those with whom I agree ideologically. I confess, too, that I also counted heads and couldn't see where you'd find a fifth vote. It is even assuming a lot to think you can get four of the eight commissioners."

"Does that mean you haven't made a decision on whether to contract the flu?" Lainy asked. "I don't intend that as hard as it sounds, Pete, but it should be easy for you to see the demand put on you was not an altruistic one."

"You're right, Lainy, but you have been active enough in politics to know that total idealists don't get past the first election. A person has to think of himself, too. I confess I did that until I saw this mornings's editorial in the *Courier*. You know, my wife's grandfather didn't have any debts, was never arrested, was kind to his neighbors, loved his country and raised an exemplary family after the death of his wife. But he was taken away to Bergen-Belsen and gassed because he was a Jew. Just because others thought they had a greater right to life than Jews. No trial. No constitutional protection. Well, in America, the preamble to our constitution says we have the right to life, liberty and the pursuit of happiness. Of course, the first is the most important, for without life, one cannot have liberty and happiness."

"The *Courier* said there was no analogy between the killing of Jews and the killing of womb babies. They deny discrimination exists against a class of people when it comes to the unborn child. But we all know the child commits no crime and is denied life without due process of law. No truthful doctor will deny that these little ones are human beings from the time they are conceived. Everyone here knows abortion is the same as snuffing out the lives of Jews, or withholding civil rights from blacks or Indians. That's why I've turned down the party machinery. That is why my vote goes to you, Connor."

We were all quiet for a moment and then we lifted our wine glasses simultaneously in a salute to Pete and then to Robb. Mama Martino came to the table with a wrapped bottle to fill our empty glasses. The rest of the luncheon was devoted to the status of Winona Smith and Clark Mathews and to the wisdom of approaching Sam Talbot on the lines drawn in the editorial.

The *Courier* helped us to look honestly at the congressional seat. I knew I must concentrate first on the mayor's race, but I couldn't help musing on the chance to go to Washington.

Was I to be a member of congress, participating in the fight for the Human Life Amendment? Was that to be my destiny?

— ★ ★ ★ —

There were seven cars in or near the driveway at Winona Smith's house. I parked my car at the curb and walked up to the front door where Winona met me. A group of young people was sprawled around her living room listening to records. As I was shown into the den, the closest teenager to my path, a blue-jeans clad redhead, whispered "Good luck" in a hushed tone as I passed, and then stared at the floor as I thanked her. This recognition was exhilerating, but more importantly, I hoped it portended the outcome of the election.

Winona was passive and distant. It made me nervous. She was waiting for a pitch, maybe a hard-sell, if I interpreted her mood accurately.

"I'm not going to give a speech, Winona. You've certainly been pressured to the point of fatigue. I would like to know, though, how you feel about this morning's editorial?"

"I take offense," she said, "when a rich publisher thinks he's paying too many school and welfare tax dollars and he decides the solution is to slay the unborn children of poor people. Yes, I know he was directing his comments at a neighborhood like mine. ....I like what you represent, Connor, but I'm getting requests from labor to team with Sam Talbot and hopefully Sonny Wallace, thereby keeping Vada Griffin alive. When Bert Peterson took away the fifth vote from Manville by his attack on George Zachman, he kept you in the race, but he also improved the viability of Griffin."

"I may have to stay with Griffin until I am released. But I presume I'll be ready for you on the third or fourth ballot, since I don't expect any progress by labor. I can't say for sure I'll come over to you on this or that ballot, but I can tell you I'm not voting again for Walter Manville. Of that you can be positive."

She never mentioned the cable TV tentacles of Al Kelder. Maybe Winona had an early indiscretion and then backed out when she realized it was truly graft and not a relatively harmless situation such as when a lunch is bought or a bottle of liquor is delivered at holiday time. When she assured me she would not be voting for Manville, she must have been informing me she had repudiated her initial association with the bribers.

Jack Clay and Lainy Ross were trying to get Clark Mathews and Sam Talbot to attend a meeting with our group tonight. When Allison Reynolds phoned the DiNapoli for a report on today's developments, she asked me to have another dinner meeting at her house. I accepted quickly. Even if neither Mathews nor Talbot attended, we had several points of strategy to examine.

The problem with which I was currently preoccupied was in deciding what to do if Manville's supporters on the city council tried to form a coalition with Sam Talbot. They already had snatched Sonny Wallace from labor. Or so it seemed.

I could be sure Winona wouldn't go over to

Manville, but I wondered if Talbot would change his vote if he were told Vada Griffin would be appointed to a plush job. That was what Griffin reportedly wanted, a good paying position. Maybe he could be made overseer of the cable television franchise. Then Kelder's placement cycle would be completed.

— ★ ★ ★ —

Allison had set an elaborate table, with candelabra at either end. Courtney took his guests into the intimate and cozy library overlooking downtown Burlington. A middle-aged man wearing a bartender's vest solicited drinks from Jack, Bart and I, the original campaign group.

Lainy was shown into the skyline room as we finished our first highball. She announced promptly that Sam Talbot refused her invitation and would not discuss his vote.

"Did you find anything out, Jack," she asked.

"I had better luck than you, but I didn't get any conversation from Mathews. He said he'd drop in to talk with us after we had eaten."

We took our drinks to the table where we dined on broiled filet mignon with mushrooms and whipped potatoes.

For the first time, the subject of cracking the Manville bloc was brought up. If we were provocateurs, we could try to exploit the well-known dichotomy existing between Wetherby and Hayden. But that again would be negative, unbecoming, malpurposed politics. Furthermore, with both of their names on the warehouse deed, their freedom to disagree had been stunted.

I quieted the group's fear of Winona voting once more for Manville. "She informed me today," I said, "that she was committed to Griffin for a few ballots and then might come over to me if Vada showed no progress. Therefore, our coalition hinges on Talbot. Now, the reason he is steadfast in his backing of Griffin is due in part to his worry that labor will not endorse him in the future, and in part to a genuine friendship with Griffin. I doubt he has any animosity for me, or for Manville."

The maid signaled with her hand to her ear as I spoke, so I followed her into the living room for a telephone call. It was Clark Mathews.

"Connor, I won't be able to make it to your dinner meeting. Please give my regrets to the hosts. Can we talk a minute?"

"Of course, Clark."

"I've been playing with the strategy of pleasing Constance by voting for Manville the first couple of ballots and then switching to you. But there's a danger my vote could push Manville over the top if my name is called out first or near the beginning of the list. The city clerk reminded me that commissioners' names may or may not be called out alphabetically."

"I paid Constance back in this past week's balloting by going with Manville. Now I want to go all the way with you. I just don't know about a majority, though."

"I can't thank you enough, Clark. That information will buoy our staff and it might strengthen their effort to ferret the fifth vote from an unexpected source."

"There is some background you should know, Connor. Ellsworth Hayden is going to start the election process again on Monday morning. He will claim he polled enough city council persons to get approval to resume the balloting. His plan is to wait until Sunday evening to notify you, Vada Griffin and any of the commissioners and deputies he did not poll."

"Some other background I'm interested in, Clark, is Sonny Wallace's purpose in apparently not intending to vote for labor's candidate. I don't care if his name is on that warehouse deed. He needs labor's help in future campaigns and he won't have it by going over to Walter Manville. The way things seem now, he doesn't have a political future."

"Haven't you heard the grand plan? It's Sonny, not Manville, who will be running for congress this fall. With him in Washington, Manville in the mayor's office, Constance, Ellsworth and possibly Zachman in the city council, Al Kelder will own a politician on three levels of government. That's important to him."

"Kelder knows the compelling interest in Wallace returning to labor, so he plans to offer the Labor Temple a goodly sum of campaign money if it will endorse Sonny for congress. He believes Sonny will be a capable contact man with the Federal Communications Commission."

"Where's all the money coming from? Is cable

television so lucrative that a franchise-hopeful can distribute a fortune to a few office-holders and candidates in exchange for bureaucratic favors?"

Clark answered me very guardedly: "It's confidential. A billion dollar eastern foundation is the silent but powerful partner in cable TV companies all over the country. It owns enough of the stock in Kelder's company to control the programing, and the kicker is that the foundation is promoting abortion through this medium. To make certain its aims are promoted, the foundation has a fund set aside for every local operator to control key politicians so as to get and maintain a cable franchise."

The subject of local gift-giving was not expanded upon by Clark. That could have been the reason why he ruled out a personal visit tonight, fearing the warehouse and free cars and boats would be discussed. He could be in a situation not unlike the one I thought Winona Smith found herself in, with an early mistake and then a revulsion for what he did and of what he had nearly become involved in.

I thanked Clark again and went back to the dining room. I decided not to burden the group at this time with such things as the source of the payola and Sonny's ambitious plan for this coming fall. We already knew Sam Talbot was our only hope for a fifth vote, so there was no need to pass on the information Clark supplied me. After Monday's council meeting, we could sit down and have a full critique.

I admitted to myself that the main objective in not telling my tablemates was to avoid dirtying Clark's name. He couldn't have been privy to all the foundation information without at some time having been an accessory.

Everyone was pleased that Clark was solidly in our fold. The satisfying aspect was that while Talbot was our swing vote, he was no more than a stalemate vote for Manville. Now, if we could only hold the four commissioners and acting commissioners we had presently. I guessed I could include Winona.

I wished I didn't have the gnawing dread that during the time Winona paid her token votes to Griffin and labor, Kelder might spring a diabolical Griffin-Manville scheme whereby Manville voters switched to Griffin if it appeared five votes were realizable that way.

The pressure must have affected my reasoning ability. It was only a remote possibility that Griffin could have been corrupted and taken from labor in a matter of a few hours or days. Yet, Griffin's original activism with labor's political wing was said to have been due to an awareness of labor's strength in the voting booth and not because of an ideological communion with labor.

My earlier feeling of uneasiness with Allison and Courtney—because of their wealth—was swept away by their graciousness. Tonight, I had a chance to thank them in front of my staff, partly for the two working dinners, but mostly for their bold success in verifying the warehouse ownership. I would take another occasion to show my appreciation to Jack, Lainy and Bart.

XVI

O<small>N THIS RESURRECTION</small> Sunday, the Son of God again was presented in triumph to the world, offering rebirth to the undeserving and unrepenting masses. Some would take up the cross. Others would use the day for gain, for despair, for harm.

The Nazarene brought intangible gifts of contentment in the finite and endless days for the morrow. The price tags read, "You must love!" These gifts would not be marked down on Monday, as they were measurably priced for all, from the factory hand and the young to the celebrated and the affluent.

The Easter Mass at St. Catherine's Cathedral was jammed with worshippers of all ages, races and economic strata. I offered the Body and Blood for all the girls and women who would not waver during this liturgical year in taking their pregnancies to term.

Although the temperature was only thirty degrees and the frozen ground was covered with a soft blanket of ivory snow, spring was slowly asserting its domination over a particularly cold winter.

After returning to my apartment and eating an afternoon breakfast, I stood at my picture window, absorbed in the view of the confluence of the Dain and Manitou rivers. A thin crust of ice forced the merging flows to a hidden union.

I should have been relaxed and sated on this anniversary of the central day in history, but I had been melancholic from the time I arose this morning.

The ringing telephone brought me to full consciousness.

"Connor," the urgent voice said, "this is Father John Andrews."

I recognized the intonation of the parish priest I had known before going to Korea.

We spoke briefly of the past before Father said he had something to discuss with me and asked if I'd come out to the small nearby town he was serving as pastor.

I should have reserved my concern until I arrived, but the seriousness in his request disturbed me. And after all, it had been many years since we had seen each other. Now, suddenly, he wanted a talk out at his parish house.

"Is anything wrong, Father?"

"It's in regard to your campaign, Connor. I've been following it closely in the Burlington *Courier* and yesterday I received a call from Marty O'Hara, Ann Marie's father."

"Ann Marie's father!" I exclaimed. "I haven't seen him for ten years or more. Isn't he still in Mason City? What does he know about our local politics?" My questions ran together.

"He usually comes to Burlington several times each year to meet his broker and he stays at the Downtown Athletic Club. After working out yesterday, Marty was standing in the shower when he overheard a comment which may be relevant to your campaign."

Before I could ask what the comment was, he enjoined me to come out to New Venice where he promised to elaborate.

Father Andrews could not see me until early evening, so I studied the Burlington budget for several hours before taking a scenic, winding, secondary highway out to St. Michael's rectory.

As I drove eastward, the evening sky caused me to think of Korea. A full moon near the horizon was impaling a cumulous cloud. It resembled the mammoth spotlight that North Korean soldiers used to ambush me two decades ago. The sentry post I had been inspecting was illumined to expose and blind me temporarily. I was fortunate to have had only a minor wound and fortunate now the memory returned infrequently.

Each time the ambush was disinterred mentally, however, thoughts of Ann Marie also were reawakened. "Are they cached in the same cerebral corner?" I wondered. It seemed that freeing one released the other.

The forty mile drive passed quickly enough even on the antiquated highway. Father Andrews was waiting for me. As I could expect of this man of several academic degrees, the walls of his study were lined with scholarly-titled books.

We were genuinely and equally glad to see each other. I hoped my shock on spotting his aging face was not noticed. As with most young people, I had no idea what his age was when I was leaving for overseas duty. My only recollection was that he had been in his vocation for a lengthy period. Now he appeared to be an old man. I was immediately impressed, though, with the quickness of his mind.

"Connor," he said, "I didn't know you were acquainted with Commissioner Wallace in Korea."

I was puzzled, but I did not deny knowing Wallace. A soldier meets so many people, some for long intervals, some in transit.

"I don't recall knowing Wallace before I became active in the Jefferson Club, a local political discussion group. What are you getting at, Father? By the way"—I said it kindly—"if Marty O'Hara is interested in my campaign, and I believe he would be, why didn't he call me instead of you? Be sure, I am not being impertinent, just curious."

"It's a fair question," he said. "There is no reason Marty didn't call you instead of me. The fact is, he did call you, but he had no answer at your place. He was on his way to New York to spend Easter with Ann Marie and her family and he phoned me from the airport. Marty left a New York telephone number in case there was anything significant to the remark at the Athletic Club. He wants to help you more than you know. But his emotion may have been one of apprehension because of the marriage between you and his daughter that never took place. To this day, he thinks of you as his own son, the son he never had. He's always avoided seeing you since then, because, for some reason, he thought you might believe he had something to do with the breakup. In truth, he still doesn't know what caused you and Ann Marie to part."

I had hoped I was going to learn what prompted Marty's daughter to abandon our long-ago engagement. Now I was more unsure than ever.

The priest continued: "I won't keep you waiting any longer for the comment Marty overheard. He did not know who Sonny Wallace was, although he now recalls seeing Wallace's picture in the *Courier*'s rural edition and reading articles about his political activity in an ecology publication. When he was toweling himself in the club's locker room, a middle aged, ruddy-complexioned man standing next to an open locker said to a fellow ten or fifteen years his junior, 'If Mullaney becomes mayor, he's going to wrest the Democratic congressional endorsement from you this fall. You realize that, don't you?' The tall scarecrow with blond hair and feet too short for his body replied confidently to his half-dressed companion: 'Listen, I took care of Mullaney when I was in Korea and I'll do it again, this time with votes!"

A thousand reflections went through my mind.

Father Andrews guessed as much, saying, "Are you trying to recall some incidents that occurred in Korea?"

"Yes," I answered, as my hands encircled the snifter of brandy he had served me.

Feeling my way, I said, "As a captain and company commander, I must have made some people unhappy. It was my duty to maintain a disciplined unit, and in order to do that, some of my soldiers probably disliked or even hated me. Getting back to Wallace, though, I can be certain I didn't meet him overseas. Honestly, I don't even know if he is from

Burlington originally. Nor do I know where he went to school. I suppose I'd be a better politician if I knew those things."

Both Father Andrews and I agreed that the shower room story did not seem like the type of bravado Wallace would fabricate.

I realized I hadn't told him about the cable television empire of Al Kelder and of Sonny Wallace's apparent involvement, so I digressed for a moment, synopsizing what information I had.

"Let's backtrack a bit further," Father said. "What happened to your engagement with Ann Marie? Weren't you in Korea when you broke up?"

"Yes, but our breakup had nothing to do with Korea. She married a guy who had never been in the armed services."

He was persistent. "Nevertheless, I'd like to hear what split you two. If I ever knew a well-matched couple, it was you and Ann Marie. When I read of her marriage to someone else, I thought it was a misprint."

"I'll tell you, Father, but I will consider it disconnected from the point we're discussing."

Father Mike Andrews poured another brandy for each of us and settled back in his chair as I recited a happy and painful narrative of my relationship with Ann Marie O'Hara, a five feet, two-inch lass with tiny chestnut eyes and a natural smile on a whitish Erin face.

"I spent sixteen months in South Korea, landing in Seoul in this kind of weather. Later, I was sent to one of the spots where the Armistice was being breached continually. I started with a platoon and by the time I was hit in the knee some months hence, I had a company under my command."

"We didn't have the Phillipine vacations the Viet Nam soldiers had. It would have been an ideal break from the loneliness Ann Marie and I knew so keenly."

"I met her through a mutual friend in my sophomore year in college and we knew soon that we had a special relationship."

"She had propriety, loyalty, warmth and many other attributes that attracted me. Maybe it was mere chemistry. I shouldn't say 'mere' for that type of chemistry is the world's glue."

"The months passed swiftly and we fell in love. Ann Marie switched to a nursing major in her junior year, so I was graduated first. She was to get her cap just a few weeks after I arrived in Seoul."

"Ann Marie proudly informed me she would have enough money saved for a down payment on a house by the time I was discharged from the Army. Being out in the boonies, I also knew that I was going to save some money."

"She had wanted to marry before I left, as did I, but I decided it would be better to wait. I didn't like the possibility of her becoming a widow, or a widowed mother. She accepted this. We had great trust for each other and knew it would help us remain loyal in our geographical separation. Our union was unconsummated, Father, but we were one."

"Before I left Fort Lewis, Washington for Seoul, Ann Marie flew to Seattle for a weekend. When we said goodbye after two and one-half days, days that whizzed by, Ann Marie took pains to promise she would always love me without reservation, regardless of whether or not I made it back."

I turned back the calendar more than I had intended, so I asked Father Andrews if he had heard enough.

"I have a little glass of spirits," he said. "I'm in my easy chair and I'm hearing an interesting story. I'll complain if you're discursive."

We toasted the present as I continued with a twenty year old memory.

"Even up near the thirty-eight parallel, the mail from Ann Marie came almost every day. She included every sort of trivia with her professions of love. I was a faithful writer, too."

"She was working as a registered nurse for over a year when her letters suddenly stopped coming. I tried to call her on a terrible overseas hookup and it didn't go through. Finally, I had the Red Cross see her when my letters were returned. They found that she was all right, but Ann Marie would not communicate with them. I didn't go through her parents. I felt that since she was emancipated, it was a matter strictly between us."

"We had intended to meet at San Francisco and be married there when I was discharged, but when I hadn't heard from Ann Marie for several months, I knew of course that she wouldn't be there."

"I had an outstanding regimental commander, Colonel John Quincy Johnson. I related many stories about him in my letters to Ann Marie and I guess that he heard countless times about her. The colonel and

I went out to dinner four or five times after we came ashore. He helped me talk it out."

As I sipped the brandy, Father asked, "Did you ever find out what caused the sudden reversal of feelings?"

"No, I still don't know what happened. After a couple of months back in the states, one of Ann Marie's friends told me she had met a quiet, unassuming fellow. Nice personality, good family man. Everything about him was a plus."

"Did you ever see her again?"

"I thought I saw her everywhere. I did a double-take at any brunette with an Irish countenance. I didn't see her in person until six years ago, fourteen years after the cessation of her letters. She was eight months pregnant and uncomfortable. We had a nice weather-type chat. Nothing more. Her husband was solicitous of my well-being. I wanted to assure him my well-being would have improved greatly if Ann Marie's expansive girth had not mocked the virginal marriage she and I once knew."

I was done and the catharsis must have been etched on my face. I hadn't thought about the relation of the story causing relief, but during all those years since the nights on the San Francisco wharf when I dined with Colonel Johnson, I hadn't spilled it out to anyone.

My reminiscing made me forget politics momentarily. But Father Andrew's alert mind remembered.

"Is it possible Commissioner Wallace figured in the cause of your breakup with Ann Marie?"

"Well, Father, I suppose it's possible but I don't know how he could have been a factor if I were not then acquainted with him. And he couldn't personally have been involved with Ann Marie in the United States if he said he 'took care' of me while in Korea."

"Wallace couldn't have been responsible for your knee wound, could he? What things went awry for you while you were overseas?"

I turned my head from side to side.

"No to Wallace causing my injury and no to anything going awry, except my engagement."

"Where are we, then?" he asked. "We haven't linked anything to Sonny Wallace in Korea, yet my instinct tells me there was something dastardly he did to you."

Father became thoughtful. "You know, Connor, many people have an advantage, albeit dubious, that you did not have. They can rationalize losses of the heart because their prime motivation was economic or social. They are pragmatists, realists. This is not necessarily satanic, but seldom do these people attain a high and aesthetic love."

"Compromised romances such as these are rived more easily because the couples' goals are materialistic. Conversely, when an ideal couple like you and Ann Marie parts, it is often a freak mistake that had been made, or there had been some type of outside interference."

Father's housekeeper was at the door of the study, waiting for her employer to finish speaking.

"I know you didn't want to be interrupted,

Father Andrews, but there is a long distance call from a Mr. O'Hara."

"That's all right. I want to talk with him."

Father gave me the study telephone and said he was going to take the one in the kitchen. He picked up the receiver and told Marty O'Hara that I too was on the line.

Marty spoke wearily. "Father John and Connor, my grandchildren are spending their first Easter without their father. Ann Marie's husband was terminally ill with cancer for nearly a year. His heart finally gave out seven months ago. She has the kids out for a ride now, so I thought it would be a good chance for me to call you."

My pulse was rising rapidly. I tried to calm myself, but with no success. The simple life I had known suddenly was becoming complicated.

Mr. O'Hara continued: "The reason I phoned was to tell you of the conversation I had with Ann Marie in regard to her broken engagement with you, Connor. I'm going to shock you, but I have to ask this question. Did you father a child in Korea?"

"Of course not, Marty," I said impatiently.

He was apologetic. "I brought it up because Ann Marie received an anonymous copy of a birth certificate in the mail while you were in Korea. There were the customary names of the father and mother. You were listed as the father and the mother's name was an Oriental one."

I was miffed. Would Ann Marie believe the writing on a piece of paper sent by a nameless person?

"Marty," I said, annoyed, "if Ann Marie wanted to know whether I fathered a child in Korea, why didn't she write and ask me? We had a long, trusting relationship. She could have found out very easily."

Father Andrews listened intently, not making a sound as he stood at the entrance to the kitchen with the housekeeper's phone in hand.

Persistently, Marty said, "Connor, she wrote twice asking you if the certificate was authenic. She never heard from you and her letters were not returned, so she felt that you received them. When she didn't get any mail from you, she wrote to the man you admired, Colonel Johnson. Being your friend and superior, Ann Marie thought logically that if he verified the truthfulness of the birth record, the information would be from a reliable source. Colonel Johnson answered by return mail, saying something to the effect, 'Yes, I'm sorry, but it is true that Connor had a child by a local woman.' With this, Ann Marie decided she would let you make the next move."

I was beginning to feel an ugly mood come over me. It was as if I were on trial.

"I'm not satisfied, Marty," I said. "For the foundation we built, she could have waited and quizzed me face to face; and if she loved me, she could have forgiven me if it had been true...and it was not true."

"She was willing to wait and talk to you in person. And, Connor, she forgave you before the sun went down on the day she received the colonel's letter. But after another month, she wrote to Colonel Johnson again, asking him to intervene with you on her behalf."

"The second letter from Johnson, with his letterhead, arrived shortly. It was a sad tale of you marrying the woman who bore your child. Named as the marriage official was a priest-chaplain. Attached to the correspondence was a copy of the marriage certificate, giving the same name for the bride as the name of the mother on the birth certificate."

"Ann Marie checked with her diocesan marriage tribunal. There, a priest said that with Orientals, a non-removable impediment to marriage called disparity of cult often is present. However, if the woman were a Christian and a maiden and they exchanged vows before a priest, the sacrament then would have been made validly in the the eyes of the Church. That was the end of the line for Ann Marie. Later that year she met and married the man that she recently put in the ground."

In a mollifying voice, Marty continued, "I don't believe for an instant that you're not telling the truth, Connor. But what I have in mind is that in some cockeyed way Sonny Wallace may have been involved, after what I overheard in the locker room. I say, let's track down Colonel Johnson."

I was agreeable to that, even though I was skeptical about Wallace causing our engagement to be broken when I didn't even know him until I became a part of Burlington politics. And even though the name of Wallace was fairly common, I didn't remember hearing it in Korea. But then, that was a long time ago.

"What you suggest makes sense, Marty," Father Andrews interjected, "but I'm afraid anything you may find out wouldn't tie in to the mayoral election, and even if it did, it would come too late to help. The mayor pro tem may resume the balloting tomorrow."

Marty O'Hara was undaunted. "I know someone at the Pentagon. Sunday or not, I will call him at home now and tell him it's an emergency. If he gets me Colonel Johnson's telephone number, I'll phone the colonel yet tonight and lay it all out to him. Maybe he knew Wallace in Korea."

"It's going to be difficult," I said. "John Quincy Johnson has to be retired by now."

I gave Marty the name of the outfit the colonel served in while he was in Korea.

Coming close to Ann Marie with this long distance call from her home unnerved me. Too many forgotten moments were resharpened.

As we closed our conversation, Marty said, "I'll do my best. Where can I reach you in City Hall tomorrow morning?"

I looked up and gave him the number of the Clerk of Court's office and then Father Andrews indicated he'd like to be the intermediary. He offered to go back and forth from the clerk's office to the council chamber while I was absorbed with the balloting; that is, if it took place tomorrow, and all indications were that it would resume then.

"One last thing until tomorrow, Connor. Ann Marie wants you to know that in all the time you've been parted, you were in her prayers every day in each of those years."

His message had a telling effect on my emotions, so Father thanked Marty for me and asked him to pass it on to Ann Marie.

Father Andrews and I talked for a few minutes after hanging up. Then I strode into the brisk evening, hurrying to my car. I made better time returning to Burlington.

XVII

The monday morning *Courier*'s banner headline read, "MULLANEY HOLDS FOUR ACES." The bylined article was erroneous in speculating that Sam Talbot was one of the four commissioners planning to vote for me. None of our information gave credence to that possibility. Clark Mathews's name was left out. The writer was accurate, though, in stating Winona Smith was going to give Vada Griffin a token vote before backing me. This concerned me, as it would hurt Winona the next time labor endorsed city council candidates.

I waited until the council's gavel time, and then took a little-used entrance to the City Hall complex so as to avoid reporters. But as soon as I neared the main floor elevators, an electronic reporter, with cameraman poised, said to me: "With Overstreet and Holloway and now Smith and Talbot, you have two Republicans and two laborites voting for you. Did you promise to cut the budget for the Republicans while telling the laborites you wanted higher wages for government employees?"

As long as it was utterly without foundation and intended only to produce controversy, I ignored the question and stepped onto the waiting elevator. Bart, Allison, Lainy and Jack were dodging media representatives outside the council chamber. Bright lights shone toward the elevator as I was asked by a brace of reporters to verify the four aces the *Courier* said I was holding.

"We have several votes, we believe, but accuracy would be served if you questioned those commissioners named by the *Courier*."

"Isn't it true you intend to use the mayor's office for a power base? Is this your stepstone to congress?"

"Is that what you think?" I asked. "Shame on you."

It was impossible for me to huddle with my campaign group, so we went into the chamber and took our seats.

"Anything new on Talbot?" I asked Jack Clay.

"No, but if we make it through today, I think you should meet personally with him. He might feel slighted. You've always sent your lieutenants after his vote."

"Good idea. Say, has anyone seen a priest roaming around here this morning?"

"Not until now," Lainy said. "I see an elderly man with a Roman collar standing in the doorway, acting as if he's looking for someone."

Ellsworth Hayden was trying to quiet the crowd that packed the oblong, high-ceilinged, deliberative room.

I hurried back to Father Andrews, who by then had spotted me. He was excited.

"Marty O'Hara really unearthed something. During the middle of the night I talked with Marty and John Quincy Johnson, who happens to be a general now. He's not retired as you thought, but is at Fifth Army Headquarters in Chicago; and right now, he is on a flight to Burlington. Marty O'Hara was to take an early morning plane from New York. They'll both be in the chamber within the hour. Is there some way you can delay the balloting? You have to hear what General Johnson has to say. It's dynamite!"

"Just a second. I'll tell Robb to slow things up, or if necessary, to walk out. Then there won't be a quorum, if Winona, Robb, Pete Holloway and Clark Mathews leave the chamber."

Robb had been watching us and met me halfway when I walked in his direction.

"Don't ask me why, Robb, but I want you to hold up the balloting by requesting a recess for one hour. If the pro tem refuses, you can gather up Clark, Winona and Pete and walk out. Then Ellsworth won't have enough council members to carry on."

Acting Commissioner Robb Overstreet was already petitioning the senior council person before I reached Father Andrews.

Hayden responded predictably. "We just got started this morning. There's no call for a recess."

The men argued for a minute or so and then Robb walked unhurriedly and confidently to the upraised level on which the mayor's seat was situated. Apparently, he threatened to take the Mullaney bloc out of the chamber if his request were not granted, as Hayden seemed to show agreement after Robb stopped talking.

"This body will take a one hour recess," Ellsworth said angrily.

Pete Holloway and Bart Countryman found an anteroom and asked the council guard to lock us in. Since only Father Andrews and I could recognize Marty O'Hara, and only I would know General Johnson, if he were not in uniform, I started to brief the guard on my latter-day guess at their descriptions when they rushed toward me, arm in arm.

It was an unrestrained meeting. Each of us tried to express the greatness of the moment.

The men explained how they had met on a connecting flight from Chicago when Marty noticed an Army officer with one star on either shoulder.

The general was resplendent in his uniform. Marty was wearing a blue striped tie with a Navy blue blazer, contrasting his whitened hair and gray plaid slacks. Both appeared to be in excellent shape. I half-expected the physical deterioration I found in Father Andrews.

When we were surrounded quickly by onlookers, I ushered the newcomers into our commandeered room and introduced them to the members of my caucus. Marty summoned me to one side of the room, saying, "Ann Marie is on her way. She had to line up a babysitter."

In an afterthought, he said, "She helped us figure this thing out. It's really bizarre."

"What's it all about, Marty?" I asked nervously.

"The brigadier claims Sonny Wallace forged his signature on those letters to Ann Marie, and, well, I'd rather have him tell you the rest."

"Marty," I said, "we're going to be short of time.

Why don't you inform the group what you found out and I'll talk over in the corner with General Johnson."

The general and I moved over to a secretary's desk and sat on top of it.

"I understand the council will go back in session shortly, Connor, so I will just give you the hard facts now and the rest later."

He paused before beginning his discourse. Then, while moving his right hand in a chopping motion, he said, "When you presided at the courts-martial of a doctor and medic for performing illegal abortions, the procurer and moneybags was not brought to trial because he deserted the Army before he was to have been arrested. As you now can guess, it was Merwin 'Sonny' Wallace. Before he went over the hill, Wallace dummied up birth and marriage certificates in your name while intercepting your mail. It was easy. He was unknown to you because he was in another company. But he was the regimental mail clerk, handling your company's mail. He stole Ann Marie's letters to both you and me, and wrote back on my letterhead, saying initially that you fathered a child and later that you married the South Korean mother of the baby. Then he destroyed your letters to Ann Marie, which also had to go through him."

"I remember when your office was having problems with the mail," I said.

"This went on for several months," Johnson continued. "He was safe, temporarily, because the doctor and medic refused to disclose how they found candidates for surgery, as you probably will remember from their trials. Sonny had used an alias with the few aborted women who would talk with authorities, so he remained undetected and free for a couple of months after the pair was convicted and sent to the stockade."

"Why would he do this to me? He never stood trial before me and I didn't even know him."

"Well, you stopped his profitable sideline and I suppose he acted vindictively for the maximum allowable sentences you handed down to his butcher friends. Then, after he sabotaged your engagement, he took off and as far as the Army is concerned, he's still running."

"Marty O'Hara and I made a call from the Burlington airport to the Pentagon and spoke with the man who told Marty last night where to find me. That fellow checked with Criminal Investigation Division headquarters while we were on the line and he found out that Wallace never was arrested, never brought to justice."

"How can you be so certain Wallace forged your signature?"

"I can't be positive," John Quincy said, "but Ann Marie and I talked for over an hour early this morning. Although it was two decades ago, she was helpful in describing the looping style of handwriting."

"Obtaining the marriage and birth certificates would have been easy. A chaplain's assistant and Wallace's medical partners in crime could have supplied the two forms. If the latter were already in jail, any office employee at the post hospital could have helped him."

"I'm so sure of him being the cause of your broken engagement, I could go into that council room right now and threaten him with several charges if he doesn't vote for you. But then, that would be coercion."

"The alternative," the general said, with a wry smile, "is to walk over and sit near Wallace's council seat. I believe he was quite tall and had blond hair. You see, I remember him. Now, let's see if he remembers me."

With that, General John Quincy Johnson sauntered into the chamber and over to the first row of seats behind the railing separating spectators from members of the city council.

One by one, Burlington's elected representatives returned to their seats, as did the audience.

The guard had reserved most of the first row on the west side of the horseshoe-shaped table for my campaigners.

Sonny and General Johnson already were staring at each other when I sat down next to the general.

"What are you and Mullaney doing together?" Sonny demanded in a vicious but panicky query.

When John Quincy remained silent, Sonny wheeled his revolving chair around and leaned his elbows on a railing, just several feet from our bench-seats. There was a din in the room, allowing the commissioner to nearly shout with relative privacy.

"Abortion is now legal, so you can't touch me on the charge of being a procurer," Sonny yelled. "As for the desertion, I'm protected under the statute of limitations."

He didn't mention the forged letters and falsified documents.

Both the general and I continued looking impassively at the scarecrow council member.

"Why don't you answer me?" Sonny sputtered. "Why are you here, Johnson?"

The longer our muteness, the more pronounced were Sonny Wallace's jitters.

Bang! Bang! went the gavel of acting mayor Ellsworth Hayden.

"The city council chamber will come to order. The first business of the council will be a resumption of the balloting for the office of mayor. There will be no more endorsement speeches. The clerk of court now will have his secretary begin the first ballot by calling off the commissioners' names, this time in alphabetical sequence."

This placed Wallace and Wetherby at the end.

I gave the guard a note to deliver to Winona. It read, "We need you on the first ballot in case there is a Griffin-Manville coalition."

She winked at me after seeing the note.

As the clerk's secretary said "Hayden" and the mayor pro tem answered "Manville," General Johnson rose slowly and started toward the open end of the council table near the citizen's microphone.

Wallace saw him and asked sharply, "Where are you going?"

Casually, firmly, the general turned and spoke over his shoulder, "I'm going to stand over here." He stopped at the citizen's rostrum.

"Do you wish to address this body, sir?" Ellsworth asked.

"Not right now," John Quincy answered, his eyes never leaving Sonny.

The second name called was Pete Holloway.

"As the acting commissioner for George Zachman, my vote goes to the next mayor of Burlington, Connor Mullaney."

"Mathews," the secretary barked.

"Mullaney."

I tried to catch Constance Wetherby's reaction, but my view was blocked by a council aide.

"Overstreet."

"I cast my vote for Mullaney."

Three votes for Mullaney, one for Manville.

"Smith," the voice bellowed above the buzz of the spectators.

"It is my pleasure to vote for State Representative Mullaney," said the commissioner from the impoverished neighborhood as she glared at Boss Kane and his train from the Labor Temple.

Almost cutting her off, the secretary said, "Talbot."

"A lot of people in this labor town are going to ask my colleagues during next fall's campaigning why their votes did not go to the union man's candidate. I'll be proud," Talbot said, "to say then that I stayed with Vada Griffin all the way."

Sonny moved about uneasily in his chair when his name was read off. Glancing first at General Johnson standing by the microphone and then looking at and fingering the bottom of his wide tie, Commissioner Wallace said, almost inaudibly, "Mullaney."

The chamber was unusually quiet for a few seconds. Then the spectators let out a collective gasp before turning the room into a wild scene of clapping and shouting.

As Marty O'Hara, Allison, the general, Bart, Jack, Lainy, the rest of my workers and other well-wishers encircled me, Father Andrews congratulated me before whispering, "There's an important personage awaiting you in the mayor's reception room."

We made our way slowly through the throng to the mayor's office. After I stepped into the carpeted reception room, Jack and Bart barred everyone else from trying to follow me.

An immaculately dressed little lady with tiny chestnut eyes and a whitish Erin face was sitting in a padded chair, sobbing softly but uncontrollably. It was Ann Marie.

"Don't cry, Ann Marie," I pleaded. "We were never really parted."

I lifted her from the chair and held her against me as I kissed her moist lips. She clung to me as a *Courier* reporter burst into the room. I motioned him away, but he inquired, "Is she going to be the First Lady?"

"That's a reasonable question," I said. "What about it, Ann Marie? Will you become the First Lady of Burlington?"

"I will, Connor."